Waves Interference Pattern

Interfering Waves are Looking Like Particles

(Refer to chapters "Waves", "Light" and "Summary")

Published by Isroel B Babayev proofreading by ProofreadingPal & Ginger software

О, сколько нам открытий чудных

Oh, how many thrilling discoveries

Готовят просвещенья дух

Priming the enlightenment spirit

И опыт, сын ошибок трудных,

And experience, son of harsh errors,

И гений, парадоксов друг...

And genius, paradoxes constant companion...

А. С. Пушкин (1799-1837)

"Humanity is going to require a substantially new way of thinking if it is to survive."
-- Albert Einstein

"Perception is reality."
-- Lee Atwater

"There is no truth. There is only perception."
-- Gustave Flaubert

"The eye sees only what the mind is prepared to comprehend."
-- Robertson Davies

"Change the way you look at things and the things you look at change."
-- Wayne W. Dyer

"There are things known and there are things unknown, and in between are the doors of perception."
-- Aldous Huxley

Do NOT call gravity pull (attractive) force!!!

Gravity *(passage)*:

On the depiction below, you can see Space-Time between planets as inflating balloons, where the same force will cause planets "A" and "B" to move toward each other and **ACCELERATE** planet "C" away from "B". (so-called Casimir effect

http://en.wikipedia.org/wiki/Casimir_effect   https://en.wikipedia.org/wiki/Cosmic_acceleration)

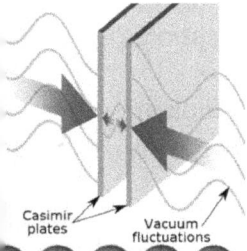

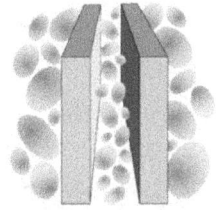

Newton's Apple

We all remember the famous story about an apple falling on Newton's head where, he claimed, the understanding of gravitational (as he called "attractive") force came to him. Have you ever asked yourself, why an apple? Is there any significance about the apple? Here we should talk about human perceptions and specifically how we (people) are so used to sketch everything on paper, which is a two-axial medium. If we split an apple from pole to pole in half, it would be easy to recognize a very familiar geometrical shape we usually illustrate on paper:

That shape would be the magnetic field as shown on the pictures below.

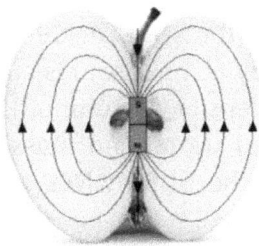

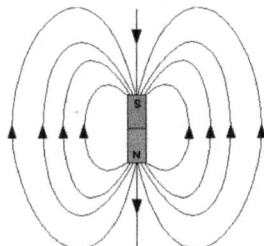

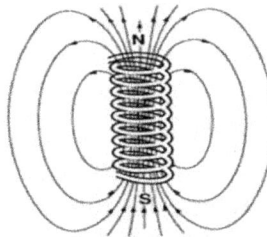

However, in 3D (FOUR-DIMENSIONAL) universe, magnetic field would look like a whole round apple.

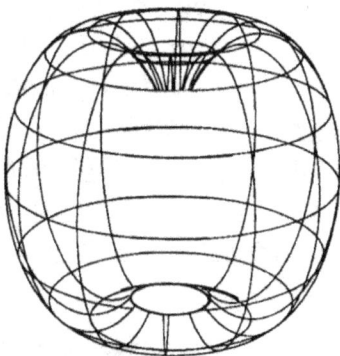

I presume that was Newton's big "Eureka!" moment, and because magnets "strive" to affix to cast iron and other metals, widely used in Newton's days, he drew parallels between so-called attraction of newly rediscovered and mysterious magnetism and mistakenly called gravity pull or an "attractive" force. *Meaning the story of a falling apple was just a ruse, most likely to confuse competition.*

[1] Robert Hooke (1635-1703).   http://en.wikipedia.org/wiki/Robert_Hooke

Space-Time (Gravity)

Atom

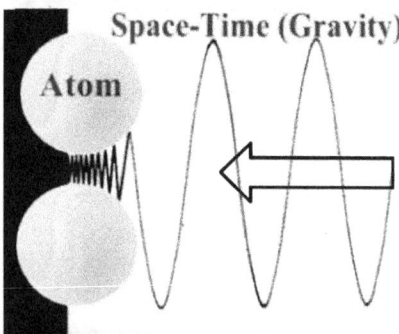

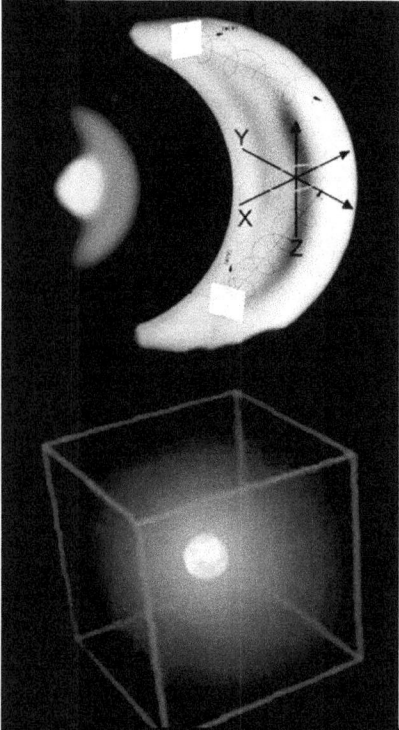

Then there was **Albert Einstein** who told us that gravity is actually a geometrical curvature of Space-Time, comparing it to a fabric, giving us another two-axial (flat) explanation, again messing with human perception. Consequently, is gravity attraction or pressure, i.e., **ACCELERATION**?

To understand gravity, let us go back to the "Big-Bang" inflation and look at the energy or motion (**ACCELERATION**) of the "Bang" itself, also known as a shock wave, and on the inevitable patterns of the <u>**waves interference**</u>.

Due to inflation or stretching of the shock wave, density became lower, and it evenly **CARVED** the ever-expanding Space-Time we perceive as our universe. Because of the waves interference, the flow of the original shock wave became smooth (chaotically balanced) and uniformed (directionally even).

Of course, some of the energy got trapped inside atoms, and as free-flowing energy encountered trapped and "curled" (matter), it had no choice but to change <u>wave length and frequency</u> (pile up around matter). The same process happened later with energy between molecules. As a result, matter started to clunk (<u>**ACCELERATED**</u>) into the giant gas clouds we know today as clouds of creation. The greater atomic density or mass, the more free-flowing energy is trapped (which is the majority of mass in an atom) and therefore greater gravitational **ACCELERATION**. Therefore, <u>gravity is NOT an attractive or pull force but an accelerative force</u> of relatively (to free flowing energy) higher density (saturation) of Space-Time. If free-flowing energy (the **SUBSTANCE** of Space-Time) is like air in terms of density, then gravity (by comparison) is air (Space-Time) under gradually increasing pressure (density, saturation). You can picture it like a traffic jam where energy piled up around mass. Just like cars in traffic trickle through a "bottleneck", the **SUBSTANCE** of Space-Time trickles through matter (waves compression). (http://youtu.be/jremIZvNDuk)

<u>Yes, Einstein's depiction of Space-Time as fabric and gravity as curvature is somewhat suitable; however, in my opinion, a more accurate (FOUR-DIMENSIONAL) explanation would be to visualize Space-Time (free-flowing energy) as a large cube of clear gelatin that you can see through. If we push some spherical object inside, it would displace (squeeze against the substance's mass) gelatin in all directions, creating regions of higher density (ACCELERATION STRENGTH) gelatin next to the object, where density is dissipating into the original saturation of gelatin, following the INVERSE SQUARE LAW.</u> (http://en.wikipedia.org/wiki/Inverse-square_law)

That curving and dissipating higher density Space-Time is Gravity.

The **SUBSTANCE** of Space-Time does have mass (dark flow, dark energy, dark matter...), and that mass exerts constant pressure, i.e., **ACCELERATION**. (http://en.wikipedia.org/wiki/Le_Sage's_theory_of_gravitation) Thus even though a majority of energy does flow through matter (WIMPs, neutrinos), heavier atoms make it flow more slowly (tighter bottlenecks), creating more gravity. For a better understanding, let us look at water inside a space-station (or shuttle). For water to remain liquid there should be an appropriate temperature and pressure. Also, gravity is needed so water can flow like we observe in nature. If we expose water to open "space", it would freeze and vaporize at once. But inside the space-station (or shuttle), there is temperature and pressure; however, there is no gravity (to be more precise, micro-gravity), and water clunks into sphere(s) and floats. It takes a spherical form because gas is pushing (**ACCELERATING**) it equally from all directions (same reason all stars and planets are spherical).

Inflating (**ACCELERATING**) Space-Time Exerts Constant Pressure

__Therefore, the same force (SUBSTANCE), call it "dark flow", "dark energy", "dark matter", gravity, inflation, mass, force, wave, flux, cold-plasma, aether, pressure, Space-Time, i.e., ACCELERATION, makes matter clunk together and move (ACCELERATE) away from each other.__ (*Einstein's "Cosmological Constant"* http://en.wikipedia.org/wiki/Cosmological_constant) To understand how, picture two gas clouds in cosmic spatial-geometry. Between them, several light years of Space-Time are pushing (**ACCELERATING**) apart; however, on all other sides, there are several billion light years of Space-Time pushing (**ACCELERATING**) them toward each other. As mentioned above, Space-Time does have mass (**ACCELERATION**), and that mass will eventually **ACCELERATE** both clouds into one, therefore creating greater density (saturation) and, as a result, greater pressure inside, which in turn begins the process of creating stars and galaxies. For example, our moon does not attract water in oceans but simply acts as an antigravity device, changing the gravitational balance (strength) of the Earth. It is always all about balance and rebalance (power) of forces and matter as our entire universe is built on a simple binary system of higher (logical one) and lower (logical zero) regions saturation (density, pressure), which are perceived by us as **PRESSURE-WAVES**. Therefore gravity is the collected (augmented, accumulated) mass of Space-Time (so-called dark matter) around and within massive objects and groups of matter (gas and dust clouds). You can view Earth like a nucleus of an atom, and gravity around it would be the electron probability cloud. We all know the effects of the shock wave in cases of being outside of it, but what if you are inside the wave? What if you are a lumpy part of the original shock wave itself? What if your very existence is based on a certain density of the SUBSTANCE? As you probably guessed, all waves are pressure-waves (i.e., **ACCELERATION**); all waves go through a process of natural decay (mathematically known as equation), or thinning, and eventually dissipate due to inflation or stretching (red shift, entropy). Finally, all waves are made from smaller waves, where each full wave is a 360° loop and where angle of inclination between zero point and pick point is always 90° when, in fact, both points are **ONE-AND-THE-SAME**, as both are indications of flip (**stop**) points. Are you confused yet? I know I am. And unless we stop relying so heavily on our human perceptions (measuring everything in terms of Space-Time) and "rewire" our brains to include the possibility of being at once everywhere and nowhere in particular, the true nature of our physical world will keep eluding us. (More in chapters "Waves", "Motion-Information", "Light", "Quantum Theory" and "Summary.")
(http://en.wikipedia.org/wiki/Gravitational_lens http://en.wikipedia.org/wiki/Supergravity https://www.youtube.com/watch?v=jremlZvNDuk)

There is a series of videos from Fermilab hosted by Dr. Don Lincoln, and in one of them, he postulates a question on the strength difference between magnetism and gravity where a permanent magnet is holding several paperclips. (http://youtu.be/5UDUNqwWuNs?list=UUD5B6VoXv41fJ-IW8Wrhz9A)

Unfortunately, what people do not realize is that it is not about the strength of the magnet but about the mass of an object. If we try to hold up an object with the mass of several dozen skyscrapers, I doubt we would be able to create a magnet strong enough to fight Earth's gravitational **ACCELERATION**. Sure, theoretically it's possible, but practically, it will waste so much energy, thus making it impossible. *__Is strength difference between atmospheric pressure and twister (tornado) surprising for anyone? Such is the difference between gravity and magnetism.__*

(Refer to chapters "Waves", "Motion-Information", "Gravity", "Magnetism", "Light", "Space-Time", "Dimensions & Spatial-Geometry" and "Summary")

Why our universe and everything we know is **ALWAYS** <u>**FOUR-DIMENSIONAL**</u>? On the image you can see three coordinate axis (X, Y, Z) of spatial-geometry. Can you choose and decide which of those axis is less important than the other two, or they all equally important? Whenever someone is describing (portraying) two-dimensional realm, for whatever reason, thinks that it would be possible to move in only two-axis, basically making one of the axis obsolete and therefore less important. Actually all three axis (spatial-geometry) plus aging-time are **SINGULAR** <u>**INDIVISIBLE**</u> **SUBSTANCE** and by eliminating any one of them automatically removes all <u>**FOUR**</u>. Just as water needs two ingridients in order to be water (regardless of its state), <u>**SUBSTANCE**</u> of Space-Time <u>**MUST**</u> incorporate all <u>**FOUR**</u> dimensions in order not to convert into something different. If we observe people on Earth from outside of our Milky Way galaxy, it would be easy to realize that we are not only in **constant and only forward** motion in aging-time but also in actual and very physical spatial-geometry. **None of us <u>EVER</u> returning to the same physical point (place) in relation to the geometry of the cosmic spatial-grid** (the matrix).

You'll read more on those subjects in section "Preface" and chapters "Waves", "Motion-Information", "Dimensions & Spatial-Geometry" and "Summary", for now, I'd like to emphasize that there is no such thing as just time. It is <u>**ALWAYS**</u> **aging-time** as part of the substance known as **Space-Time**, and what is perceived as time is actually timing, also known as rhythm or clock. Everything we know is based on rhythmic fluctuations including (and in no way limiting to) music, dance, computers and all living organisms (biorhythms). (http://en.wikipedia.org/wiki/Biorhythm) All single cell organisms are based on biorhythms, but they do not have clocks similar to the computer clock. The ONLY "source" of the order would be the average numbers of the quantum fluctuations (quantum harmonic oscillations http://en.wikipedia.org/wiki/Quantum_harmonic_oscillator) which are diminution in overall coherence due to Space-Time inflation (stipulating the rate of natural decay) and therefore must be constantly replenished. Our entire existence is based on the regular (rhythmic) "bits" as it is a form of resonance. This subject is very controversial and can NOT be explained unless you'll STUDY the entire theory, and accept it as a singular (not to be mistaken with unique) occurrence. (Chronobiology http://en.wikipedia.org/wiki/Chronobiology)

Energy is a singular (standalone) continuous substance, and force is a geometrical shape (digitized due to interactions) of that substance, where gravity is a dissipating accumulations of the force, and magnetism is a twister of the collected substance, and also can be considered as a "point" force. Therefore, protons and surrounding mass are lumpy points of the substance, we call matter, and minerals are compressed assortments of the substance known and perceived by us as Space-Time. This subject sensationally complex in its simplicity, and the only way to comprehend it to the full extend is to change <u>**OUR PERCEPTION OF REALITY**</u>.

http://scholar.google.com/scholar?q=rhythmic+quantum+fluctuations

Isroel B Babayev

ISROEL B BABAYEV

Unified Theory of Most Everything

&

Subconscious over Conscious Mind

Micond.com

A journey from Science Fiction and into the Science Fact

"If I have seen further it is by standing on the shoulders of Giants."

-- Isaac Newton

From Author:

The "OUR PERCEPTION OF REALITY" is an eye opening educational aid, reference guide and visual assistant to demonstrate in simple, non-technical, terms the emergence of our universe, processes and forces we experience and observe in our daily lives. It shows how slight, philosophical change in perception as well as interpretation of physical laws would have a profound and everlasting effect in understanding and accepting our reality. Throughout the book I'm using examples and illustrations from our everyday life, as well as thought experiments that are easy to follow and duplicate for practically anyone, with or without scientific training.

__While this book explains most physical processes, it is, in fact, all about the psyche and falsified perceptions, where often human conscious mind driven by subconscious phobias is refusing to accept the obvious, only because from the early age it was conditioned to expect something different. For example; do you know there are no such things as push and pull or even attraction and repulsion? And it gets even weirder, where force (a force and not four as perceived) and dimensions are not what we expect them to be. Therefore, I'm urging you to find a lot of patience and conduct your own research before giving up even if what you are reading seems to you like a complete gibberish.__
(To read this theory online with full color images and related videos visit http://www.Micond.com)
In the course of my life I studied a great deal of different subjects such as electronics, physics, chemistry, biology, programming, music, dance, cooking, psychology, philosophy in general as well as of martial arts and more..., and my greatest strength has always been to find commonalities in fields that are, at first glance, distinct and unrelated. It is my most cherished hope to help people to achieve the level of scientific and technological wisdoms where clean and affordable energy would be available to anyone[1], anywhere[2], anytime[3] and at any amounts[4] and such technologies like antigravity, warp propulsion, asteroid mining, terraforming and colonization of planets are everyday reality, as it should for the "Type One" civilization, precisely because Space-Time, mass, matter, energy, force, waves, pressure, acceleration and even motion-information, in actuality, are ALL - **ONE-AND-THE-SAME**.

__Theory is NOT about any religious dogmas, it is neither confirms nor denies any creationist speculations.__

Content:

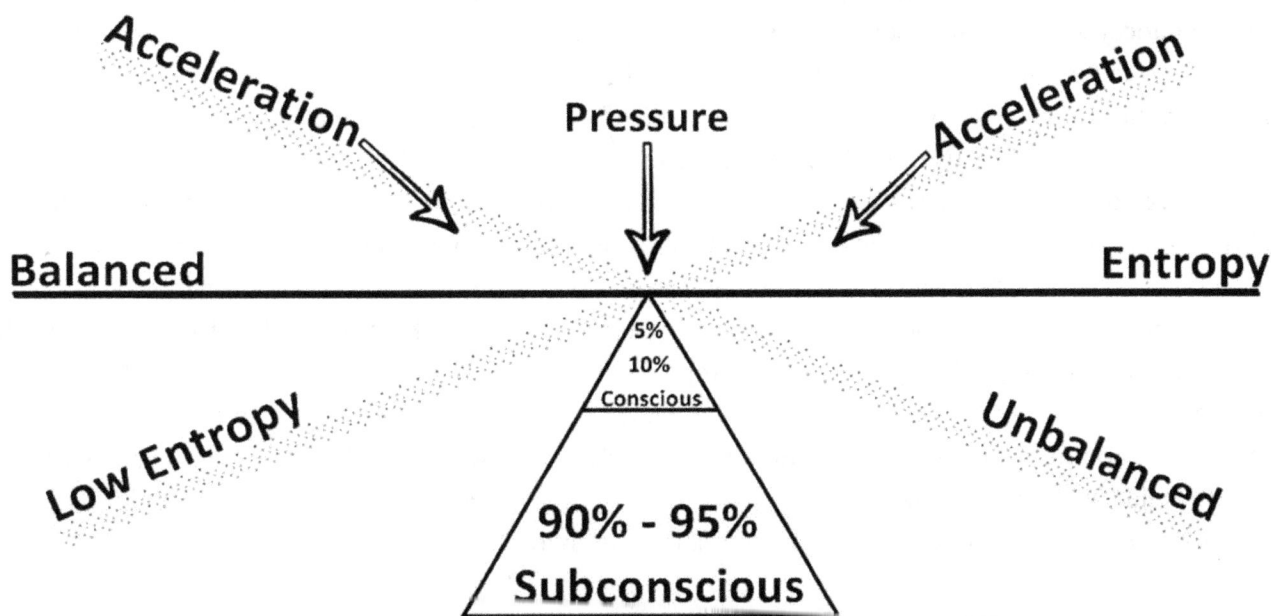

*"You cannot teach a man anything; you can only help him **discover it in himself**."*

-- Galileo Galilei

Preface:

How and why this theory was written:

First of all, I cannot stress enough the importance of reading and understanding the **ENTIRE** theory! It took me over 35 years of studying various, seemingly unrelated, disciplines and over 7 years conducting experiments to discover the true nature of our reality and it is absolutely impossible to explain energy[1], force[2], mass[3] and matter[4] without understanding the entire process of emergence and human perceptions. All mathematical and physical formulas and every law, regardless if it has been confirmed by experiments or not, is created based on our human perceptions, and current understanding or acceptance of our reality. There is a documentary hosted by physicist and mathematician Brian Green, where M.I.T. Professor Walter Lewin talks about consumed food not being quantized. While quantized means to limit the possible values to a discrete set of values, in my opinion, that is a good example how perception is influencing our understanding of reality. Actually, consumed food is quantized, but it simply not as obvious as it is with sub-particles. You cannot eat more food than your stomach allows, even if you push yourself as hard as possible because, eventually, you will throw up. And you also cannot eat less than daily calorie requirements because, eventually, you'll starve to death. Yes, it is hard to see and accept the similarity, but remember; the very word "quantized" came from word "quantity". It might appear like I simply took existing theories jumble them together and put my own spin. In actuality, every conclusion and hypothesis expressed are logical extrapolations of seemingly simple and supposedly well understood natural occurrences of wave dynamics (interactions). ***The references giving here are only to show my quest for the confirmations of ideas and conclusions conveyed, and to indicate the general direction science and physicist are progressing.*** Unfortunately, our human senses (vision, hearing, sense of touch, smell and feelings) are not very sophisticated (nor precise) and, as a result, our own perceptions are often lying to us, allowing our subconscious mind to control rational, conscious thoughts. Therefore, it's not enough to achieve absolute precision in mathematical formulas and experiments; it is also **extremely** important to be very precise with words we choose to describe events in classical physics and especially quantum mechanics.

For example; whenever someone uses words "field" or "fabric" your mind creates impressions with surface area, but if we use word substance (substantial or a lot of) it understood as something of immersive volume which is more or less distributed all around us. There will be an extensive explanation about dimensions in chapter "Dimensions & Spatial-Geometry", however, this perception of our reality is so important to understand and remember and so counterintuitive to our very essence of life that I felt it is important to mention it in "Preface". As you are looking at this text on the "flat" surface of the computer screen or book page, you are compelled to consider it as a two-dimensional "flat" realm where you can move only up-down (vertical) and left-right (horizontal). At the same time you know that ink, paper, computer screen, every subatomic particle and even "empty" Space-Time itself (so called Higgs field concept http://en.wikipedia.org/wiki/Higgs_mechanism) have depth, therefore it is ALWAYS **FOUR-DIMENSIONAL** (three-axial spatial-geometry plus aging-time http://en.wikipedia.org/wiki/Axial).

Why is this so important? Well, because in two-dimensional "world" (substance) there is no such thing as Space-Time therefore motion, in our conventional understanding, is simply NOT possible. Everything we are, and everything we do is **ALWAYS** **four-dimensional** and **NEVER-EVER** two or even three! We are, the entire universe, in constant, uninterrupted, physical motion forward not only in aging-time, but in actual and **ALWAYS FOUR-DIMENSIONAL SPACE-TIME**, where **SPACE IS TIME AND TIME IS SPACE!!!** It's those kinds of seemingly trivial imperfections of our perceptions keeping us from realizing and understanding the true physical nature of our reality (https://www.youtube.com/watch?v=Z8HO5DGZcM0). Let say you have a painting of the car parked on the street where you can see only the front of the car. Obviously following common, human, logic you'd call that painting two-dimensional because if it was a real car on the real street you'd be able to walk around the car and see, among other things, its back site, and that is precisely where our perception is lying to us. The only reason we have those kinds of expectations is because we analyze reality (the universe) from our large and "solid" view. But while there is no denying of large, seemingly solid, structures we also know that all objects are constructed from extremely small entities we call atoms and all those atoms are held in place by magnetic fields. Furthermore, modern physics teaching us that all atoms are 99.9999999999999% so called "empty" Space-Time, making all solid objects, looking (from subatomic view) more like a mesh with extremely large holes. To us, large, complex entities, there is a distinct difference between actual car and painted one, but for the subatomic "particles" they are both just another **FOUR-DIMENSIONAL** structure, an object, with all three-axial spatial-geometry and aging-time where, unlike us, they ("particulates") can travel in any directions with little or no distinction between paint, canvas, metal and other minerals, liquids, gases and/or plasma. If we take mesh rolled tightly into several layered tube and immerse it into a liquid, it would get saturated like a sponge. Same way all physical objects are saturated (soaked) by a substance we recognize as energy, and that energy, due to "Big-Bang", is already geometrically shaped into the force. I can certainly understand the reluctance of many people (especially physicists, cosmologist, astronomers, mathematicians...) to even consider to explore non-mathematical (philosophical) approach, after all, there is entire "army" of very smart, well-educated scientists, engineers and even amateurs who are, very successfully, have been relying for so many years (generations) on well proving calculable approach, but, sometimes, in theoretical physics it feels like those people simply adopting experimental results to desired expectations. For example; the way scientists at LHC (Large Hadron Collider) detect new particles is by observing trail of changes they make in the detectors, because those "particles" decay rates are almost instantaneous. However, in case with the Higgs-Boson (so called mass particle), it has been determined created during the early stages of the "Big-Bang" by observing changes left over by other particles and then performing lengthy, complex calculations. And now we have worldwide mass "hysteria" on particularized approach where people absolutely refuse to see so called "particle" and full-wave as being **ONE-AND-THE-SAME**.

In psychology there is such thing as crowd or mob mentality, where it teaching us that it is easier to influence large group of people rather than an individual, and so, people all over the world keep "stepping on the same rake" ("reinventing the wheel" and writing same formulas over and over again, but in different variations) trying to make sense of two competing theories which are seemingly incomparable not realizing that it is their own **perceptions** and therefore **expectations** that are at fault.

(http://en.wikipedia.org/wiki/Crowd_psychology   http://en.wikipedia.org/wiki/Large_Hadron_Collider)

Isroel B Babayev

Observe those formulas below;

$$\vec{F} = m\vec{a}$$ http://en.wikipedia.org/wiki/Force

$$E = mc^2.$$ http://en.wikipedia.org/wiki/Energy

$$W = V \cdot A$$ http://en.wikipedia.org/wiki/Watt

$$\mathbf{p} = m\mathbf{v}.$$ http://en.wikipedia.org/wiki/Momentum

As you can see they are all practically (philosophically) the same. In all of them mass is multiplied by some kind of acceleration while calculating Force, Energy, Power and Momentum.

$$\text{Intensity} \propto \frac{1}{\text{distance}^2}$$

Within our **FOUR-DIMENSIONAL** universe the above formula, indirectly could be considered as theory of everything, precisely because everything dissipates following the **Inverse Square Law** which is exactly how **ACCELERATION** is manifesting itself.

http://en.wikipedia.org/wiki/Inverse-square_law
http://en.wikipedia.org/wiki/Brownian_motion
http://en.wikipedia.org/wiki/Acceleration

Book 1.   Prologue:

Subconscious over Conscious Mind

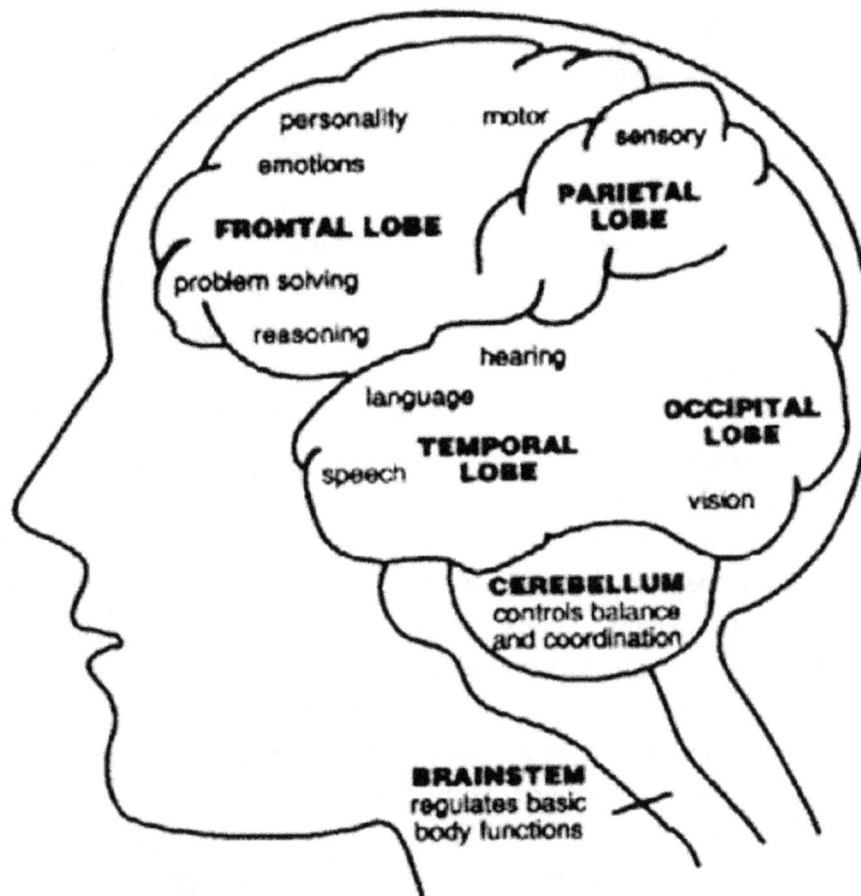

*"I need one of those baby monitors from my subconscious to my consciousness so I can know what the hell I'm really thinking about." -- **Steven Wright***

C'est la vie:

"Such is life": This is perhaps one of the most profound philosophical wisdoms ever expressed, as only by accepting the reality, regardless how uncomfortable, weird and/or unfair it really is, we can gain enough knowledge to overcome any adversity and to transcend the "mysterious".

The "Book 1. Prologue" is directly related to the entire discussion on perceptions of our physical reality, which will be main subject of analysis for "Book 2. *Unified Theory of Most Everything*", and is part of my other book where I intend to expose the appalling enormity and dastardly, disgusting hidden practices regarding subconscious mind manipulation, which is used (and in most cases abused) to keep people in "darkness" and therefore under control. These techniques, by far, not recent (or original), and have been used (applied scientifically, rationally) for many generations of the current era as well as far into humanity's distant past. (Neuro-Linguistic Programming http://en.wikipedia.org/wiki/Neuro-linguistic_programming)

If you are familiar with the subjects of human psychology and animal behavior, you'll probably make distinction between subconscious and so called unconscious mind. That distinction was intentionally omitted to minimize confusion. (http://en.wikipedia.org/wiki/Subconscious   http://en.wikipedia.org/wiki/Unconscious_mind)

In the course of our lives we have to deal with many unknowns, most of which are frighteningly challenging and beyond our control. Nature is often indiscriminately cruel and demanding. Disasters and dangers like hurricanes, tsunamis, lightening, floods, plagues, earthquakes, volcanoes, asteroids, predators, and many others…, natural or otherwise, force us to seek refuge in our own rational, conscious mind, where, it seems, we are in complete control and free to make our own, supposedly carefully planned and well thought-out, <u>conscious</u> decisions. This fundamental concept of being in control of the situation creates false, and for the most parts ignored, feelings of assurance and security, even power. In many aspects of our lives, we rely heavily on our abilities to rationalize the situation and to find, again as it seems, best solutions to the befalling problems. Unfortunately, we rarely, if ever, realize how much our thoughts and decisions are being controlled by our subconscious phobias and preconceptions. What is even more dreadfully offensive to us is to realize (or even consider) that our subconscious mind can be manipulated (intentionally or otherwise) to such an extend that it would output into the conscious part of the brain ideas, perceptions, <u>feelings</u> and expectations that are accepted by us as our own thoughts, visions, and understandings to such degree where we would be deeply and **<u>honestly</u>** offended if someone dared even to try to point to the errors of our ways, thought patterns, and **<u>expectations</u>**. What makes it even more heinous, is coupling the above technique with **<u>artificially created</u>** dangers and therefore intentionally (profitably) forcing fears to such degrees where people would willingly risk their life and lives of others, including their own children.

As mentioned, this is part of another book, so I will not go, in this version, into great details on the techniques themselves and will instead concentrate on the scientific discussion of the human mind and subconscious-to-conscious interactions.

(http://www.nlpu.com/NewDesign/NLPU_WhatIsNLP.html   http://www.neurolinguisticprogramming.com)

I'd like to remind you that self-education is the best and most gratifying way to discover and gain knowledge by sheer extrapolation and comparing of seemingly unrelated fields and topics.

I urge you to find and learn as much as possible from materials outside of this book and, as always, draw your own conclusions.

Let us first understand our so-called "actual reality," the world that is all around us.

Unfortunately, it only seems like we live in the world that is surrounding us, when in actuality we reside in the realm constructed (composed) by our own brain. All the information we receive via sensors is nothing more than **external agitations** of brain synapses, where the brain reconstructs what appears to us as reality. For example: human eyes have only three receptacles for color, those are known as R.G.B. (red, green, blue) basic colors, but the average person can distinguish many different colors and millions of shades. That is because our brain is sophisticated enough to recognize intensity for each of the three basic colors, and extrapolate (calculate, recreate and fulfill) the missing information.

The problem, is that reconstruction isn't completely based only on external agitations, but is also influenced by our genetics, dreams and prior experiences going all the way back to our mothers' wombs and then forward through childhood, adolescence, teenage years, and so on.

But that's not all, because perception of so-called reality is also influenced by minerals chemical imbalances, nerve degradations, parasites, bacteria and viruses affecting cells throughout your body. And if all of that weren't enough, the mind is also influenced by internal clocks (plural) that sometimes do not agree with each other, creating falsified realities.

Personality disorder, dissociation, amnesia, depersonalization, derealisation, identity confusion, and identity alteration are some among many mental illnesses recognized by contemporary medical science where people are partially or completely disconnected with surrounding reality.

However, as modern scientists are realizing more and more, you do not necessarily have to be mentally ill to reside in your own world. Have you ever watched how small children play? They exist in their own realm for the most part, often mysterious and disconnected from the outside world. Not only we do not find such behavior alarming or critical, but we actually encourage the idea, considering it a vital part of the childhood "magic". Many adults got famous and make good living, by inventing so-called "realities" which are far removed from our realm. Who of us didn't enjoy the story *"Alice in Wonderland"*, where cat can smile and disappear, mushrooms and other items make her grow and shrink, and where complete absurdity is perfectly normal behavior, because it was a dream, and dreams don't have to make sense; they do not require a continuation of the story and can be as jumpy as they "desire".

Each of us resides within own minds (conscious-subconscious), and the only reason why most of us on the same "page" is because we have been conditioned from the earliest age to perceive so-called reality according to generally established standards. These are the accepted ideas of normality, and cognized behavior is explained as, "Do what is done by the majority".

In an experiment with children, ten of them were asked to identify black and white objects on a table. Nine of those children agreed ahead of time to lie, identifying the colors in reverse. When it was time for the tenth, uninitiated child to name objects by color, even though the child knew the truth, he/she would name them in reverse.

I have two dogs and they love to play catch, but, every now and then, they would run and search for the ball while it is still in my hand, because their prior experiences create in their brains a falsified image (action) of the ball flying through the air, so that the dogs actually follow the imaginary ball's ballistic trajectory and then run to search for it while being confused and switching from, trusting the eyes mode to sniffing.

Have you ever noticed that the loudest and most aggressive dogs are actually the smallest? That is because they are always subconsciously frightened and that makes them consciously find solutions to compensate for the physical inadequacies. Because all dogs have wolves as common ancestors and every "fiber" of dog's being is "screaming" to be bigger and stronger. There is a fable, by *Ivan Andreyevich Krylov* called *"Elephant and Pug"*, where a tiny dog is barking and attacking uncontrollably a huge elephant, creating an alarming situation of up-startling the elephant and thus actually endangering itself and others even more, because dog's frightened, subconscious mind is forcing the dog to defend itself by preemptive strike, not realizing that it is actually achieving the very opposite impact, as startled elephant is **whole lot** more dangerous and unpredictable.

Mentally, subconsciously, we are not too dissimilar from animals and practically all of our decisions, one way or another, are based on subconscious phobias, whether we realize it or not.

There is a well-known phrase from *Hamlet*, "The lady doth protest too much, methinks" (III, ii, 239), which is often rephrased and repeated as, "Me thinks thou doth protest too much", meaning those who protest too loudly or aggressively are the most guilty of what they are protesting. During the Prohibition years in the United States, there was a female activist, who was the most vulgar and aggressive in her anti-alcohol "crusade" because, as discovered later, she was an alcoholic herself and subconsciously was afraid that she would be exposed.

As it is often the case, a guilty and/or frightened subconscious does make people do things that are more detrimental to the person than the circumstances themselves. Why is that? Because a person can lie and manipulate other people, and they can even lie to their own conscious minds, but we can **NEVER! EVER** lie to our own subconscious. *(The ultimate "all-seen" eye not on the top of the pyramid as depicted on the American (U.S.A.) one dollar bill, but it is under "water", somewhat hidden, and for the most parts unknown. This, hopefully, will make sense later.)*

That always scrupulous (vulnerable to outside influences, physical or otherwise) subconscious mind also regulates all of our vital organs and glands, including all senses and muscle groups, which, in turn, means that you can actually **physically** do things and not even know about them. We've all heard stories about sleepwalkers, and many of us actually talk and move in our sleep. I've been observing my dogs sleep, and as they undoubtedly dream about running and having emotions, their limbs will jerk, as though they are running for real, and they will also vocalize these feelings, which often can be interpreted as joy or frustration.

There are cases of people being in sound mind, and not experiencing personality disorder, who have physically done things (reacting) and not even realizing they've done something.

There is a documentary about blind man who jumped away from hurtling bus not even realizing that there was danger and his body reacted, saving his life, which is a good example of the subconscious mind's ability to control the physical body (including the senses) without registering it in the conscious part of the brain.

Once I tried for several months to learn how to juggle tennis balls, when I suddenly realized that my hands started catching falling objects before I understood what was happening. There were several cases when glass goblets or other fragile objects could fall off a table or other surface top to their demise, and my hands, unknown to me, would catch those objects before I consciously comprehended the situation. There is such thing as peripheral vision (http://en.wikipedia.org/wiki/Peripheral_vision) which is, for the most parts, communicates directly with subconscious, rarely registering in the untrained conscious mind. The same is true for some of the subsonic and ultrasonic vibrations, meaning our sensors and subconscious minds are capable of registering much wider spectra of waves.

As you know, boxers, wrestlers and other athletes train daily for several grueling hours, repeating similar exercises, moves, and techniques to reprogram their bodies to the point where the subconscious mind takes over these acquired abilities.

It is a common practice among professionals who deal with the human mind to describe these processes (conscious/subconscious) as being like a triangular iceberg floating in the water, where only 5–10 percent of it is visible above the surface and 90–95 percent is hidden under water. That depiction is an illustration of all processes happening in the conscious and subconscious parts of the human brain, respectively. There are processes happening in your mind as you read this paper of which your conscious mind is unaware, and these are not only about regulating and managing bodily functions, but also involve our sensors. Those sensors are capable of detecting a much wider vibrational spectrum of both "electromagnetic" and physical waves (like picking up subsonic vibrations thru bones), and processing them in the subconscious part of the brain without ever registering it in the conscious mind.

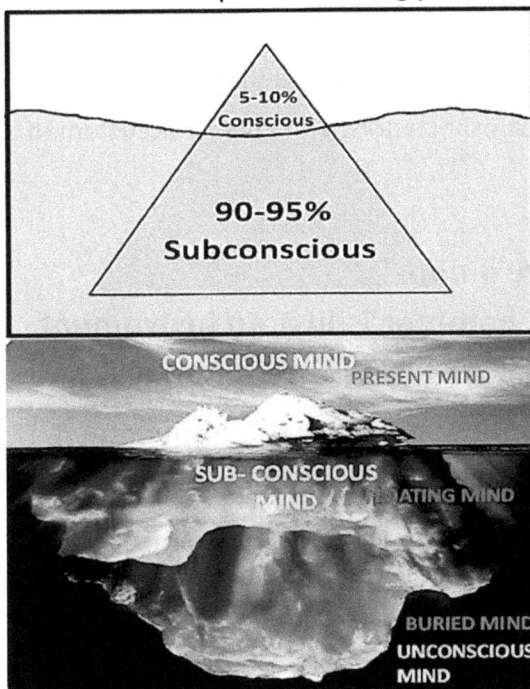

We are surrounded by living organisms that actually do not even know that they are alive (self-unaware) like plants, viruses, bacteria, insects, fish, reptiles and many more, and yet, they do respond to dangers, forage and/or hunt for food, adapt to changing environments, mutate into new strands (often a lot faster than we can keep-up with), and procreate.

Do you remember about the blind man who jumped away out of the hurtling bus and didn't even know about it? In that same documentary, there is a story about another guy who lost his subconscious association due to a prolonged coma. Once out of the coma, he looked at his parents (dog, house), saying, "Yes, you do look like my parents (dog, house), but you are not them." Basically he perceived everything recognizable as empty shells without substance. And then there was another man who lost his conscious memory but retained his subconscious one. When his father came to pick him up from the hospital, he said, "I do not know who you are, but it feels like there is a connection and I should know you." In this situation, there was a substance (we perceive as emotions and feelings), but no shell.

The above examples and many more give us a clear indication of how the subconscious mind overwhelmingly dominates the conscious one to the point where we don't even suspect it unless the specially trained conscious mind learns to overcome emotions, expectations, and perceptions.

Whether we want to or not, our conscious minds constantly test new information and ideas against previously acquired knowledge, where subconscious minds are "firing" alerts from the depth of negative emotions and feelings, as radical advances often go against what is familiar and comfortable. We determine if innovative ideas make any sense by measuring them against our current understanding and acceptance of physical reality, which creates certain expectations based entirely on human perceptions. Unfortunately, that baggage of knowledge often hinders instead of being used as the foundation, a "stepping-stone", such conditioning becomes a blinding wall that prevents us from observing the obvious only because it is unexpected and **DECEPTIVELY** simplistic.

In the entire history of truly innovative (sometimes radical) ideas, those who dared to go against conventional <u>perceptions</u> **were at first ridiculed, laughed at, and treated like shortsighted morons or even criminals, all because those "Giants", as called by Isaac Newton, actually knew more than others and were not afraid to "speak their minds".**

In conclusion, I'd like to emphasize that, realizing or not, our subconscious minds **overwhelmingly** dominates over the conscious ones, and unless we learn to be **patient**, inquisitive, and tenacious **way beyond conventional persistence**, able to overcome established expectations and change accustomed **perceptions**, the true nature of our reality will keep eluding us.

As stated by the famous phrase;   (http://en.wikipedia.org/wiki/Law_of_the_instrument)

"When you are a hammer, every problem looks like a nail."

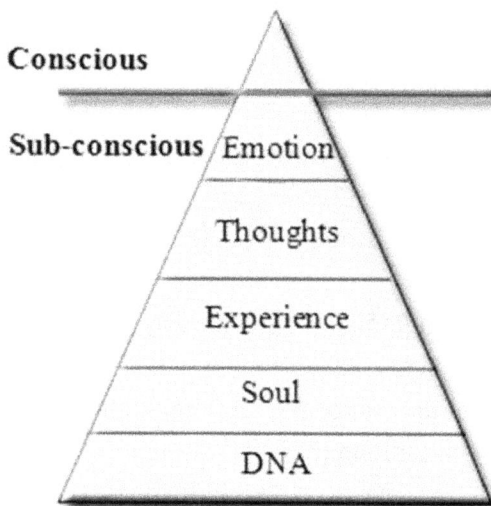

But remember, the **hammer is just an instrument,** NOT the main structure. While mathematics and geometry are truly languages of the universe, all languages are only tools to convey ideas and express emotions. Furthermore, every problem requires a suitable tool, in size, shape, and strength, and the only way to realize if our selected "tool" is appropriate is through acquiring the proper **PERCEPTIONS**.

"The subconscious is ceaselessly murmuring, and it is by listening to these murmurs that one hears the truth." -- **Gaston Bachelard**

Book 2. The Theory:

Unified Theory of Most Everything

From Single Energy into Single Force and to Single Theory

Accelerations, Perceptions & **Waves Dynamics**

or

"Escargot law of extremely slow motions."

(Most - is also Russian word for the Bridge)

"The difference between average people and achieving people is their perception of and response to failure." -- **John C. Maxwell**

Table of Content

*"What we observe as material bodies and forces are nothing but shapes and variations in the structure of space. **Particles are just appearances**. ... The world is given to me only once, not one existing and one perceived. Subject and object are only one. The barrier between them cannot be said to have broken down as a result of recent experience in the physical sciences, for this barrier does not exist. ... Let me say at the outset, that in this discourse, I am opposing not a few special statements of quantum physics held today (1950s), I am opposing as it were the whole of it, I am opposing its basic views that have been shaped 25 years ago, when Max Born put forward his probability interpretation, which was accepted by almost everybody. I don't like it, and I'm sorry I ever had anything to do with it."* -- **Erwin Schrödinger: The Interpretation of Quantum Physics.** (http://en.wikipedia.org/wiki/Schr%C3%B6dinger_equation http://en.wikipedia.org/wiki/Erwin_Schr%C3%B6dinger)

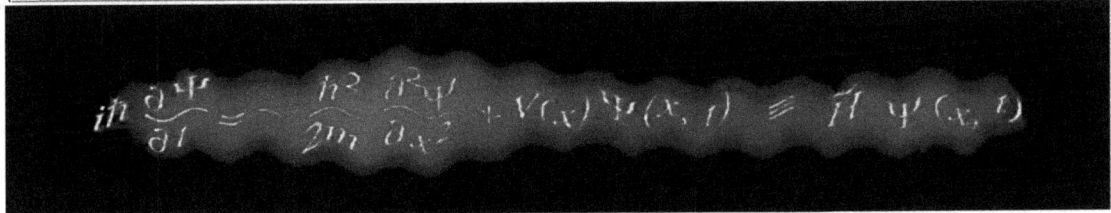

$$i\hbar \frac{\partial \Psi}{\partial t} = -\frac{\hbar^2}{2m}\frac{\partial^2 \Psi}{\partial x^2} + V(x)\Psi(x,t) = \hat{H}\,\Psi(x,t)$$

I. Abstract:

"Perhaps, the greatest challenge for us, humans, is humility."

While above phrase has been repeated throughout the ages, it keeps finding the most unusual ways to teach us, not only about spiritual concepts (**not to be mistaken with religion**), but as it turned out, also very physical substance of our existence. As I was conducting an extensive study of physical processes and modern interpretations of our mathematical views on classical and quantum mechanics, it got more and more apparent how intricate and unbroken our physical world is interwoven with everything we would call metaphysical or intellectual, as all that we are is **one-and-the-same**. While this theory will explain most forces and processes we encounter in nature, it is almost ironic to realize how much convincing is needed to explain concepts as trivial as waves or acceleration, and to show how simple change in **perception** could have a profound effect not only on experiments we conduct, but also change the very quality of life itself. It is our, human, psyche that forcing us to stubbornly deny ever-present "physical" connections to the universe and consequently to each other, thus dividing everything on particles without even considering a possibility of **full wave and particle actually being one-and-the-same**. (Concept known as wave-particle duality http://en.wikipedia.org/wiki/Wave%E2%80%93particle_duality)

While this theory is seamlessly combines both relativity and probability concepts into one "Unified Theory of Most Everything", it is precisely because everything is made from same **substance**, one cannot give full explanation on a single physical event or force without referring to the entire process of emergence. **To fully understand the concept, it is absolutely imperative to go through entire theory, connecting events and processes, looking for the confirmations outside of this paper, and draw your own conclusions. The theory itself is a loop, made up of smaller loops.**

I realize that construction of this abstract is in complete violation of classical abstracts. All I can say, read this theory in its entirety, and then, read this abstract again, and you'll understand why that is, and why, I put so much emphasis on seemingly trivial occurrence such as pressure-waves, i.e. - **ACCELERATION**.

"The most incomprehensible thing about the world is that it is comprehensible."
-- Albert Einstein

II.   Introduction:

The theory is based on understanding, or more precisely **revised perception**, of energy, Archimedes lever (circles), Newtonian laws of motion, Einstein's special and general relativity, quantum mechanics, string and "M" theories, Higgs field concept (http://www.youtube.com/watch?v=JqNg819PiZY), dark energy, dark matter, dark flow, **waves dynamics** (actions-reactions), theory of big rip and works of Tesla. (If you are not familiar with some of those concepts, I urge you to learn as much as possible as we would need that knowledge as a **foundation**.) Theory will explain (unify) what is (definition of) motion (acceleration), information, energy, gravity, magnetism, electricity, strong and weak nuclear forces, waves, particles, mass, matter and dimensions. This theory dismisses charged particles. In fact, there is no such thing as charges (nor particles) but only fluctuations in "spin directions", as well as density/saturation (which in itself is a charge and you can consider it contradiction number one) and as a result, pressure/speed, and trajectories. In basic terms, it is question of balances and saturations. The purpose of this theory is to demonstrate existence of forces (two-dimensional or metaphysical properties or entities) we encounter in nature daily and yet not fully comprehend them as "standalone" units (substances), and also to show how some laws of physics were misinterpreted and therefore misunderstood. The theory will seamlessly unite all fundamental forces into one "Super Force" as well as fuse two competing theories into one "Super Theory". **From single energy, into single force and to single theory.** In short, this is an exploration of accelerations, perceptions & waves dynamics, as part of the informational expansion and permeation throughout two-dimensional medium we label Metaphysics.

<u>It is very important to keep in mind that any reference to particles, quarks, strings, loops, helixes or conical logarithmic spirals should be considered as virtual values that do not actually exist in reality. Just as computer interface exists so we, humans, can communicate with binary computer language, interpreting sets of logical ones and zeroes into shapes, colors, numbers, letters, pixels and pictures, so do particles, quarks, strings, loops, helixes or conical spirals describe not actual but virtual units (metaphysical arrangements also known as motion-information). Moreover, the binary system itself is also a mathematical interface and actually represents high and low statuses of so called square waves. And if you are familiar with electronics, all types of waves are representations of differences in voltage (pressure/speed) called amplitude, wavelength and frequency. Following same logic, voltage in electricity is same as pressure in classical mechanics making all information and physical reality into simple differences in saturation of motion-information, experienced by us as pressure-waves or more appropriate - ACCELERATION.</u> (More in chapters: "Waves" and "Motion-Information".)

Newton's Apple
We all remember the famous story about an apple falling on Newton's head where, he claimed, the understanding of gravitational (as he called "attractive") force came to him. Have you ever asked yourself, why an apple? Is there any significance about the apple? Here we should talk about human perceptions and specifically how we (people) are so used to sketch everything on paper, which is a two-axial medium. If we split an apple from pole to pole in half, it would be easy to recognize a very familiar geometrical shape we usually illustrate on paper:

That shape would be the magnetic field as shown on pictures below.

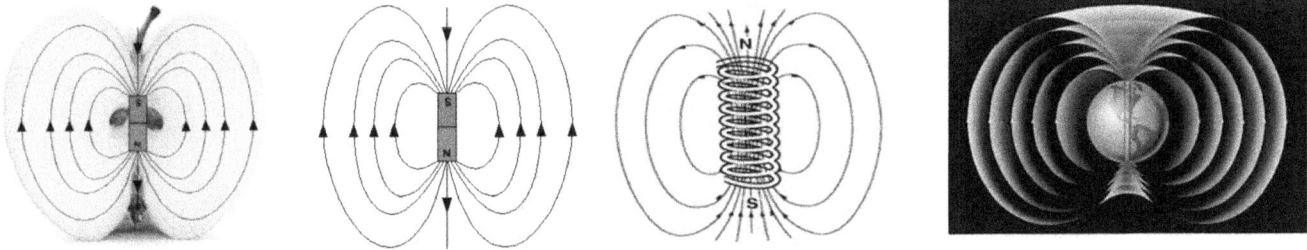

However, <u>in 3D (FOUR-DIMENSIONAL) universe, magnetic field would look like a whole round apple</u>.

I presume that was Newton's big "Eureka!" moment, and because magnets "strive" to affix to cast iron and other metals, widely used in Newton's days, he drew parallels between so-called attraction of newly rediscovered and mysterious magnetism and mistakenly called gravity pull or an "attractive" force. *Meaning the story of a falling apple was just a ruse, most likely to confuse competition.*

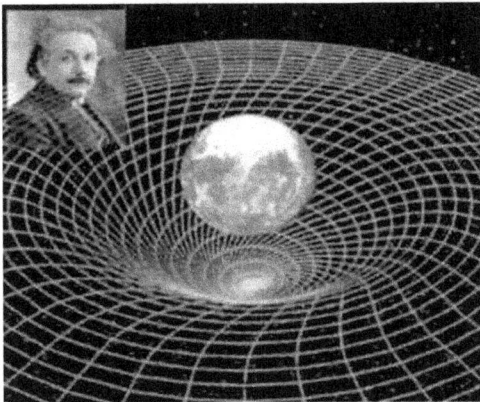

Then there was Albert Einstein who told us that gravity actually a geometrical curvature of Space-Time, comparing it to a fabric, giving us another two-axial (flat) explanation, again messing with human perception. (For more information on gravity, magnetism, and spatial-geometry please read correlated chapters.)

I'm not trying to change laws of physics or proof both Newton and Einstein wrong, however, interpretation of the law and human perception can and often do give us wrong understanding of our physical universe.

As you probably aware in American (U.S.A.) judicial system all courts exists to force the law, and only the U.S. Supreme Court exists <u>solely</u> to <u>interpret</u> the law.

<u>Interpretation of the law, any law, is a fundamental concept in our quest to understand the universe and subsequently, to understand ourselves.</u>

Archimedes Spiral

http://www.mathdb.org/articles/archimedes/e_archimedes.htm http://en.wikipedia.org/wiki/Archimedes'_screw

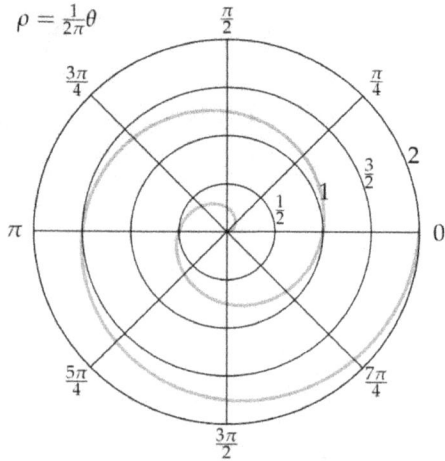

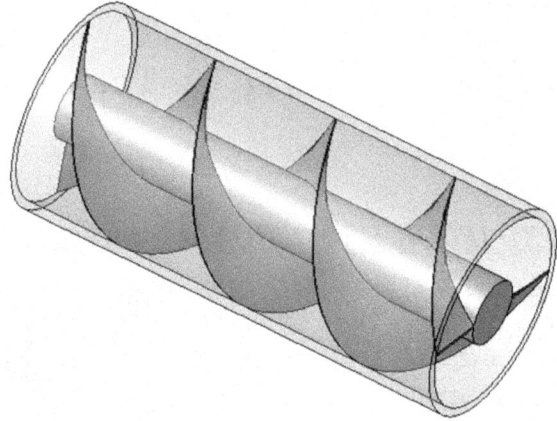

Spiral Waves Interference Patterns

*"It is entirely possible that behind the <u>perception</u> of our senses, worlds are hidden of which we are unaware." -- **Albert Einstein***

III.   Perception:

Let us talk about perception, as everything in this universe is interconnected.

In my hand I have ordinary, trivial (boring) battery. These days we all know how to use it. I personally had an experience where I purchased toy for a 3 year old, and while unpacking batteries for the toy, child kept pointing finger telling me: - "This needs to go there!"

Now, let us fantasize traveling back in time and give this battery to Archimedes. (http://en.wikipedia.org/wiki/Archimedes   http://en.wikipedia.org/wiki/Archimedes'_twin_circles)

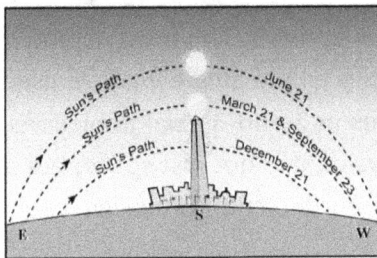

Would he know what to do with it? Would he understand its purpose without explanation? What if I give him stunt gun and batteries and ask to defend himself, again, without explanation? Most likely he'll throw them at me probably aiming into my eye. What if I take a flashlight and in front of Archimedes add batteries and turn it on? Surely he'll try to explain what happened from the technological acceptance of his period. Now, let us travel further back in time and do same with a flashlight for a caveman. Positively he would care less how it works, as long as he can use it to his advantage. As you know from history, *Giordano Bruno* (http://en.wikipedia.org/wiki/Giordano_Bruno) was burned alive and *Galileo Galilei* (http://en.wikipedia.org/wiki/Galileo_Galilei) was forced to renounce his believes, and spent the rest of his natural life under house arrest, all due to false perceptions and dogma precisely because if you sit outside watching motion of the sun, you'll observe as it seemingly moves around the Earth from East to West. Sure enough, these days, we know it isn't true (even though some would stubbornly argue otherwise) and yet, modern physicists rely on observational experiences of so called "particle" behaviors postulating concepts such as uncertainty principles, standard models, symmetries and more... Our perception of the reality is based on our current knowledge of nature. What is possible and impossible, real or fiction, even perception of Space-Time is based on current knowledge and understanding of the universe. Therefore, I would like you to keep an open mind and, just like a caveman, *do not **obstruct** your perception by the baggage of knowledge*. **Of course, we'll need that knowledge as a <u>FOUNDATION</u>, but the main "structure" would have to be rebuilt.** Also, during the presentation, I will constantly contradict myself and it would look like I oversimplify things. In fact, contradiction and simplicity are the keys to understand our reality. I'm sure we all experience contradiction in our lives, and some would say, that our very existence is a contradiction on itself. And simplicity, well, let us look into electronics. People first created telegraph, telephone, radio, radar, television, and then, simplified it into an "ON"-"OFF" switch. Our computers and all digital electronics are nothing more than a vast collection of simple switches. Also, let us not forget, that we were created from relatively simple single cell organisms.

Keeping above in mind, let us begin the journey, and, like Alice in Wonderland, discover just how incredibly deep (and therefore utterly shallow) the "rabbit-hole" is actually goes...

"Since there exists in this <u>four-dimensional</u> structure [Space-Time] no longer any sections which represent "now" objectively, the concepts of happening and becoming are indeed not completely suspended, but yet complicated. It appears, therefore more natural to think of physical reality as a <u>four-dimensional</u> existence, instead of, as hitherto, the evolution of a three-dimensional existence."
-- Albert Einstein

IV.   Waves:

We, usually, depict waves on paper like a sine wave and visualize them as we observe on the surface of the water; however, all those depictions are two-axial. If we could see electro-magnetic waves emmiting from radio antenna, so called "three-dimensional" (geometrically shaped), waves would look like inflating balloons within inflating balloon and so on... Furthermore, as we look on crests (picks) and troughs (valleys) regions of the water waves, we would say, crests regions (down) is water and troughs regions (up) are lack of water. At the same time, we know that air contains some water we call humidity and we are quite literally swimming (among other things) in the ocean of gases and water vapors. Moreover, human body itself is up to **70%** of water. Just because saturation of given medium is extremely low and/or almost non-detectable (unrecognizable), doesn't mean it does not exist. Thus, in reality, waves are uninterrupted and alternating (propagating) regions of higher density (pressure) and lower density (saturation) substance (energy). It would not be possible to breathe inside crests regions of water, but we can breathe inside troughs regions. Also, as you can see on below wave depictions, it is possible to create waves of wave. The most common example would be the Frequency Modulation (FM) radio where single wave is used to create multiple channels. So far, we looked at waves in 2 and 3 axial depictions, however, according to **Albert Einstein** and modern physics, it is not just space, but a **four-dimensional Space-Time**, and that means the proper depiction of waves would be like conical **spirals** as you can see on pictures below.

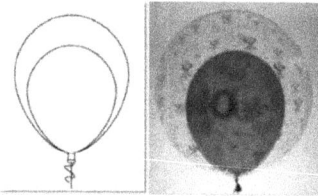

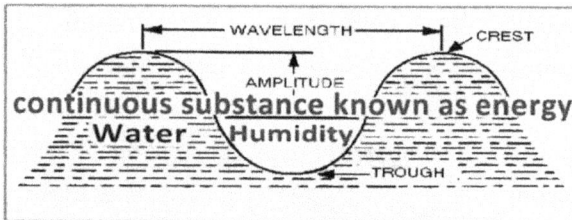

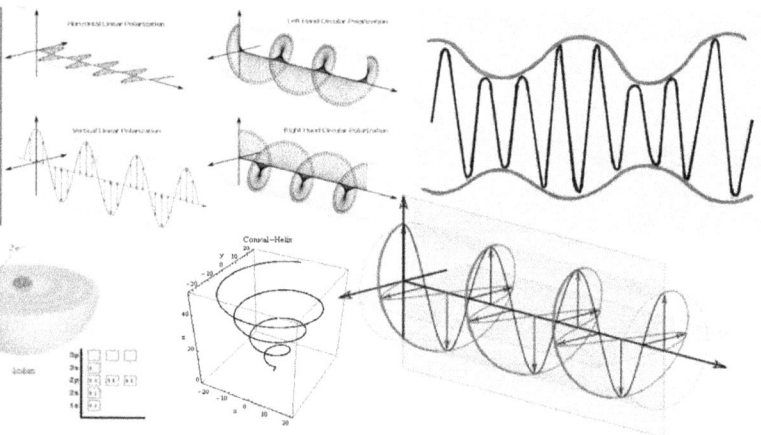

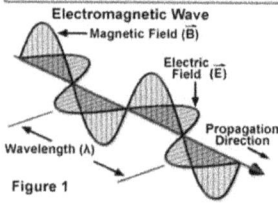

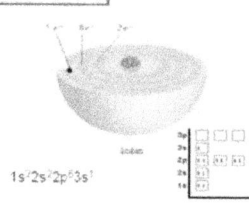

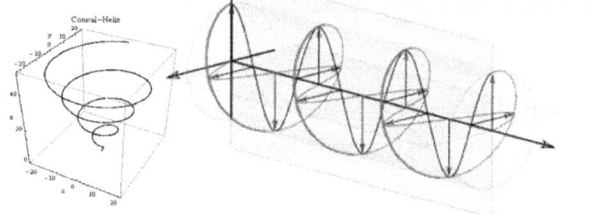

We are always stating that vacuum cleaner "sucking" air and dust, when, in reality, all it does is creating a lower pressure region and air around (atmospheric pressure) is "pushing" (forcing) or more precisely **ACCELERATING** itself into lower pressure, also known as low density (saturation) region. Without atmospheric pressure (acceleration) vacuum cleaner would never work, just as your car would never start if the pressure inside cylinders during ignitions would equal to the outside pressure.

Believe it or not, but it only feels like we inhale air, in actuality, all we do is expanding lungs (lowering inside overall saturation) and atmospheric pressure **FORCING** (**ACCELERATING**) available substance inside. Please remember; **ALL WAVES ARE PRESSURE-WAVES** (more in chapters "Gravity", "Light" & "Summary") and **WAVES CANNOT BE FORM WITHOUT SUBSTANCE!** This is true for waves in solids, liquids, gases, plasma (flux) and/or fabric (**SUBSTANCE**) of Space-Time. Without substance, it would NOT be possible for the radio waves (and all other "electromagnetic" radiations) to form and propagate. Waves do NOT travel through substances as we do. It is a propagation or domino chain effect.

(http://en.wikipedia.org/wiki/Domino_effect   http://en.wikipedia.org/wiki/Chain_reaction   http://en.wikipedia.org/wiki/Quantum_tunnelling)

We can characterize full wave as having spherical geometry and spiral structure. And please remember; <u>wave action is a transmission of ONLY the information and not the substance</u>. Following this logic, we can conclude that your body, this computer (book) and all matter can be viewed as crests (collection) of energy waves and Space-Time around us as troughs of same energy waves (more in chapter "Mycelium Field Universe"). Jumping ahead, I would like to point out that wave is both, continues and particle (full wave geometrically shaped sphere) (http://en.wikipedia.org/wiki/Matter_wave), and I'm not only talking about waves of some matter medium. The force itself is a <u>four-dimensional</u> wave and you'll read more about it in chapters "Motion-Information", "The Energy", "The Force", "Gravity", "Electricity", "Magnetism", "Light". I must also debunk another misconception of waves depictions where they are predominantly depicted with "zero" line across, dividing the wave on positive and negative regions. Actually, waves don't have zero points and that line is an indication of balance between opposing density concentrations ("charges"). Even if the wave is "destroyed" by another with 180° shift, the resulting so called "neutral" substance doesn't disappear and, as a whole, could be at higher or lower density in relation to other fields. (http://www.phys.uconn.edu/~gibson/Notes/Section5_2/Sec5_2.htm) Whenever your battery "discharges" it doesn't actually loosing mass (energy), but simply and gradually transfers from unbalanced into a balanced state. Yes-yes, some of it (tiny portion) does radiates out in the form of heat as batteries "produce" electricity by chemical reactions, but the overall volume is the same and is replenished by ambient radiations. As shown by Antoine Lavoisier in his famous experiments where he proved that mass always remains the same which is the undisputed core of modern thermodynamics concluding that energy cannot be destroyed and therefore, as it seems, cannot be created, but, surprisingly, **One does NOT always walks with the other.** (Antoine Lavoisier http://en.wikipedia.org/wiki/Antoine_Lavoisier)

❖ **Two-dimensional** or circular (non-spherical) full wave at only 180°.

This concept will make more and more sense, especially much-much, <u>much</u> later, as you'll read (study) chapters "Quantum Theory", "Summary" and Appendixes. For now I would like to review scenario presented by Stephen Hawking in his book and video, where he described how "energy" can split on so called "positive energy" and "negative energy". He starts with huge "endless" flat field where someone wants to create a hill and would have to dig a pit-hole, where extracted material is used to raise the hill, and resulting pit-hole "cavity" ("negative energy") would always equal to the "positive energy", which is, evidently, should be a good description of the 360° full wave. Unfortunately, he did not consider another possibility where material needed to concoct the hill is collected at tiny (less than subatomic) amounts across entire seemingly "endless" field. In this case the hill ("positive energy") will be achieved without any "visible" changes (drop) throughout the entire field. **"Tiny drops make the ocean."**

"Nothing happens until something moves." -- **Albert Einstein**

V.   Motion-Information:

For over the past 325 years we have been successfully using Newtonian laws of motion, and it would be very foolish to dispute the basis of "classical mechanics". Never the less, there is always room for improvement especially when dealing with human perceptions. As   mentioned,   there   is   no   point reinventing the "wheel" and write (invent) formulas; instead let us concentrate on philosophical approach of understanding motion. What if I tell you that all motions are circular (like conical logarithmic spira**l**s) in nature and the beginning is always the end and vice-versa. We encounter these conically looping **spirals** every day of our lives without giving a second thought. For example; moon loops around the Earth, but Earth itself loops around the Sun, meaning moon actually making spiral loops in cosmic Space-Time, where solar system loops around the center of our galaxy and galaxy progresses in Space-Time, still, Space-Time itself is expanding (stretching), we call that expansion inflation. You can apply the same logic from infinitely small (including Space-Time) to infinitely large. There is a wonderful lecture video on quantum entanglements by **Leonard Susskind** at Stanford University (http://www.youtube.com/watch?v=0Eeuqh9QfNI TimeLine: 0:45:00 - 1:00:00) where he talks about quantum unitarity of information and how if you start journey from point "A" and move to point "B", to point "C", to point "D"... eventually you must always arrive to a starting point (in our case "A") because otherwise, as you trace steps backward, you are losing part of information where information, **within Space-Time**, can never be lost. It is a loop which also means "Beginning" is always the "End" and so on... Now, I'll give you another example where you'll see how not only any motion plays by the same rules, but also can be viewed as a bridge (more in chapter "The Bridge") between the theory of relativity and quantum probability theory. In fact, you'll see how both words, relativity and probability (potential), are basically two sides of the same coin. Jumping ahead, I should also mention that it is wrong to call electricity and magnetism electromagnetism for the same reason why you would never call wind currents and twister (tornado) windotwister or windotornado.   (More in chapters "Magnetism" and "Electricity")

Below you see drawings of basic AC generator, sine wave diagram and a pendulum.

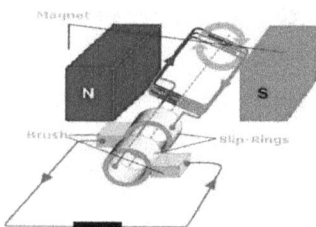

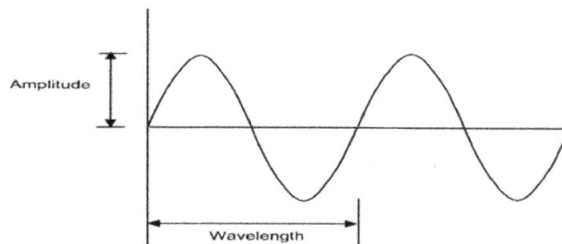

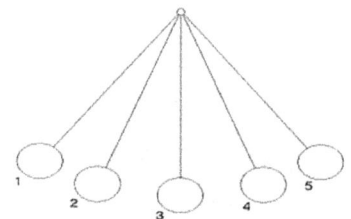

Each full cycle of electrical sine wave (wavelength) corresponds to full circle (360°) of mechanical motion of the generator. It's like mechanical loops are mirrored by electrical loops. However, same sine wave can be used to mirror mechanical pendulum motion, regardless of how far from the center point pendulum moved on each side. Look at pendulum picture above and trace full swing by following numbers, 3-1 (first quarter of the circle or 90°), 1-3 (second quarter of the circle or 180°), 3-**4** (third quarter of the circle or 270°), **4**-3(**four**th quarter of the circle or 360°). If this concept is confusing, just break single full wave on **four** stages along with mechanical motions of the generator and/or pendulum. You can view it as **FOUR** stroke engine. (Keep in mind number **FOUR** as it's permeates our entire reality

and we'll discuss it in chapter "Dimensions & Spatial-Geometry" http://en.wikipedia.org/wiki/Four-momentum)
For now, please make sure you understand how all three drawings above actually descriptions of same 360° loops. And because we are in constant motion throughout cosmic Space-Time, each loop is helical or spiral or a combination of both. As mentioned, there are infinitely small loops and infinitely large loops as well as extremely fast and slow motions. There are crystals in caves that taking millions of years to grow just a few millimeters, but they are growing, and that means motion. We are also observing loops in nature, fashion, music, politics, and so on… There is a famous saying, *"Everything new is well forgotten old"*. (http://en.wikipedia.org/wiki/Loop_quantum_gravity) Any straight line is a part of a circle and every circle is a part of the spiral, where series of spirals creates an appearance of a straight line, and we just "closed" one more loop. We all remember Archimedes words about lever: - *"Give me a place to stand and I will move the Earth"*. The work of lever is well understood and there are mathematical formulas to calculate its effect. However, have you ever wondered, why condition to gain extra power occurs **ONLY** during circular motion? The advantages due to acquired leverage by circular motion, especially well-known, understood and used in many martial arts such as Japanese "Aikido", Korean "Hapkido", Russian "Systema" and many others.

http://www.youtube.com/watch?v=1mkKhn53L68&feature=g-vrec   http://www.youtube.com/watch?v=zBlAGGzup48

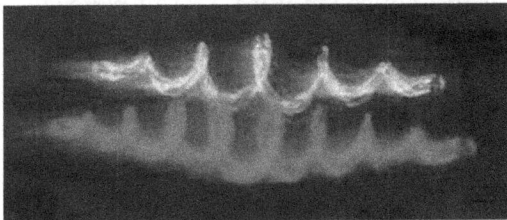

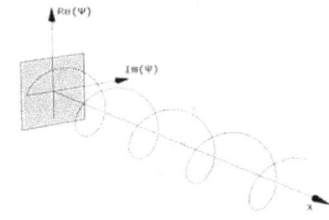

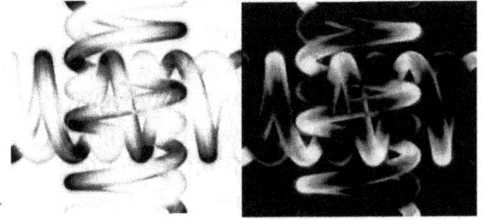

On the pictures above, you can see some examples of spiral motions, including cases where those motions crisscross throughout each other (in all directions at infinite amounts), creating appearance of spheres. Please remember, we are talking about virtual entities which, unlike physical, can actually go through each other with minimal or no interactions. The reason for such fluidity is because motion-information in actuality a **TWO-DIMENSIONAL** entity also known as metaphysical. Just as Space-Time **one-and-the-same**, motion and information are also **one-and-the-same**. A two-dimensional substance, such as motion-information, is lacking the concept of Space-Time as well as viscosity. Meaning it is, at once, everywhere and nowhere-in-particular. Just because you are reading in this paper something new or outrageous doesn't mean this is the only source. There is a great possibility that other civilizations on distant planets or even earlier Earth civilizations discovered same information and technologies. It's very possible that as you reading this paper, in some distant galaxy race of intelligent snails study physics and what known to us as "Newtonian laws of motion", known there as *"Escargot law of extremely slow motions"*. Information is ever-present, and anyone at any point of Space-Time has ability to obtain it. And yet, it is nowhere as we do not have readily available, physical source to acquire it. Data in books and other media, including this paper, is simply a reflection of our, human, perceptions. Whenever you look at your reflection in the mirror, you observe only partial data about yourself. Your reflection can be distorted by curved or broken surface; it could be adjusted by colored filters and light intensity, and so on… Motion-Information can be also expressed as a single word, for example: "Change" or "Action", as each outlines two narratives. Let say there is a chameleon, and it can mimic only two colors (two states of quantum bit or qubit http://en.wikipedia.org/wiki/Qubit). As it receives directive – "Change", it actually obtains two narrations. First one is intellectual, and the second is kinematic. Following this logic, we can conclude that motion-information is two-dimensional (metaphysical) entity (substance) which, for reasons we can only guess (could be resonance/harmonics), was transferred (shifted) into a four-dimensional substance or force (we call **acceleration** (inflation) and experiencing as pressure), thus, creating (carving) our four-dimensional Space-Time. **However, this shift wasn't the one we call "Big-Bang" Inflation.** Yes, Space-Time **one-and-the-same**, just as you constantly moving forward in aging-time, you are also moving in spatial-geometry by the same amount, and can be viewed as virtual (conically spiral) flow of inflating balloon, known and experienced by us as pressure, or more accurately **ACCELERATION.** (More in chapters "Flip-Flop Continuity", "Quantum Theory", "Dimensions & Spatial-Geometry" & "Summary") (http://www.youtube.com/watch?v=5iZ1-csQFUA)

❖ **Interactions** (Wavelength & Frequencies): (http://en.wikipedia.org/wiki/Wavelength)

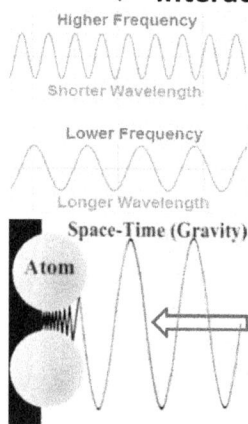

If you take, for example, tennis ball and allow it to accelerate (drop) down from some height creating action of falling object, it will hit the floor and bounce up. You might say the gravitational acceleration "down" is redirected "up" (with some loss of energy). However, if you don't catch the ball, it will reach a certain height, **stop**, and repeat action-reaction pair where each repetition would manifest as a decrease in wavelength and increase in frequency. Those changes in wavelength and frequency are always inversely related and true for all interactions including wave interferences. As you probably notice I'm using a lot of plurality that is because we are discussing very complex and therefore massive substance known to us as Space-Time, gravity, dark matter, dark energy, mass, pressure, aether and finally **ACCELERATION. The very occurrence of decreased wavelength and increased frequency is denoting <u>higher saturation (density, pressure, acceleration rate)</u> and as a result, higher rate of interactions, where it leads to more Actions and Reactions**, therefore even higher density and so on, and we just got one more example of the loop.

❖ **Rogue wave:** (http://en.wikipedia.org/wiki/Rogue_wave http://en.wikipedia.org/wiki/Interference_(wave_propagation))

Have you ever asked why tsunami waves near the coast are so much larger and more violent than the waves in the open ocean? That is because as waves encounter the shoreline they have no choice but to pile up, being accelerated (upward) by waves from behind (effect known as resonance). But what if in the open ocean out of 3 waves the middle one, for some reason, would suddenly collapse? Then, wave in front, while having momentum, would also start to collapse, creating standing "wall" of water ("standing" waves http://en.wikipedia.org/wiki/Standing_wave), meanwhile wave behind, supported (accelerated) by other waves, would experience same effect as waves at the shoreline, piling up and creating a rogue wave. Collapsed wave means lower frequency, higher amplitude and therefore longer wavelength. But the rogue wave not only goes up, it's also **curling on itself**. <u>Curling</u> is a natural process, as full wave and a spiral circle are actually **one-and-the-same** and wavelength is a distance between coils. (More in chapters "Mass & Matter", "Dimensions")

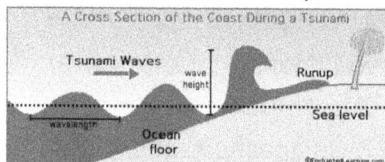

❖ **Entropy:** (https://en.wikipedia.org/wiki/Entropy http://en.wikipedia.org/wiki/Entropy_%28information_theory%29)

The entropy, as a general rule, is considered a measurement of disorder (hidden information), when, in fact, it's the other way around. You see, we, people, like when things are concentrated (unbalanced). We take the ore, refine it, put thru chemical and thermal processes in order to compress and create steel or other materials, and when it rust or decay, from our point of view, it goes back into state of disorder. However, if we look at entropy from the natures (energy) perspective, it is actually going from disorder into chaotic (self-arranged) order, or more precisely, from high and low saturation regions into a balanced state. Whenever we write mathematical equations we are balancing left and right sides. It is, in fact, a seesaw, where success is measured by total and precise balance. We, humans, see our very role in life as constant accumulations of wealth, influence (power), materials and intellectual possessions. We measure success or failure thru concentrations and accumulations. Those values are so deeply buried into the very essence of

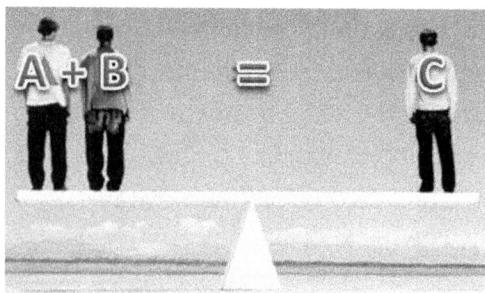

our psyche that we even assign charges to elementary particles and understand mass not as a force but as accumulations. There will be more discussions on mass, particles, energy and force; however, if you'll analyze any power to its very core, you'll see that they all based on a simple principle where high pressure (saturation) region forcing itself (accelerating) into a low pressure zone, equalizing both in process.

❖ **Holographic Principle:** (http://en.wikipedia.org/wiki/Holographic_principle)

One of the latest "novelties" in quantum mechanics is a theory where entire universe (multiverse) portraits as information, stored, like a hologram, on flat sheet of two-axial surface. While, personally, I do not champion any explanation or concept that expresses notion using word "flat", precisely because in our minds, it immediately invokes wrong perceptions, I would like to point out the overall direction modern science and physicist are progressing. Motion-Information is a two-dimensional substance permeating throughout all dimensions, because all of them are derivatives or smaller segments of same constituent. Please remember, in our universe everything has depth even if it is outside of our understanding, invisible and untouchable by us, humans. (More in chapter "Inside the Cocoon") (http://en.wikipedia.org/wiki/Digital_physics http://www.youtube.com/watch?v=2DlI3Hfh9tY)

❖ **Potentials:**

If you throw a pair of dice you'll know, with complete confidence, the range of numbers would always be between "two" and "twelve". In quantum mechanics that range of "potentials" known as probability or "uncertainty principle". By the very act of playing and throwing the dice, you are becoming a potential winner or loser. Basically, it means, the action is already taken, but out-come is unknown. The actions that created our universe, our galaxy, our solar system and us is already taken, but are we find the wisdom to progress further or destroy ourselves over trivial bickering and human greed is unknown. The point I'm trying to make, is that "uncertainty principle" is a part of our everyday life, and in so called "classical" mechanics we refer to it as "multitude of potentials".

❖ **Two vs. FOUR-Dimensions:** (Please refer to section "Preface")

Whenever people look at pictures, drawings on "flat" screen, they usually refer to those as two-dimensional, while knowing with **absolute certainty** that, paint, pencil or pen strokes, as well as the canvas itself, still have depth even if it is only one atom dip or less! Moreover, we also aware that all objects (including ink) are moving in aging-time (degrading and decaying), meaning, everything, no matter how "flat" or shallow, is **ALWAYS FOUR-DIMENSIONAL** and **ALWAYS moves in ALL FOUR-dimensions**!!! That is precisely why **Albert Einstein** called it *Space-Time*! There will be more discussions on dimensions especially in chapters "Space-Time", "Dimensions & Spatial-Geometry", but for now I'd like to point out that everything around us, including Space-Time itself, is **FOUR-DIMENSIONAL** and **any physical motion inside two-dimensional substance is simply NOT possible**.

❖ **Motions & EMotions:**

Have you ever asked yourself why sugar dissolves faster in hot water and slower in cold?

Or why mechanical agitation of water would speed-up the process even faster?

If your answer; heat and all other forms of radiations, including waves in all four states of matter, just another form of *mechanical* agitation, you'd be completely right. There is absolutely no difference between all known mechanical motions and so called electromagnetic motions. And if you have a hard time to cope with the idea, learn how a microwave oven heats water (https://en.wikipedia.org/wiki/Microwave_oven).

All forms of motion would be perceived by us as kinetic energy, including all types of emotions. Your moods your emotions are just another manifestation of very mechanical agitation. I can certainly understand the reluctance of many people reading this theory to accept the idea of motion-information being very physical (two-dimensional or metaphysical) substance and existing as so called "standalone entity", however, misery likes company, and to that confusion I would have to add one more, probably shaking the very foundation of physical knowledge on conservation of energy. You see, even though the laws of thermodynamics on conservation of energy somewhat (**predominantly**) accurate, in actuality, our entire universe (including us or multiverse or field or membrane) exists for one and only one purpose; and that is to *create*, yes *create*, more energy. Every rock, every grain of dust, every billionth of the micron of so called "empty" Space-Time, is in constant pursuit of creating more energy. A process where energy seemingly coming out of "nothing" known in quantum mechanics as quantum fluctuations (http://en.wikipedia.org/wiki/Quantum_fluctuation   https://www.youtube.com/watch?v=ltK8aR9uHW0). But it gets even weirder, because **as long as created energy within Space-Time (basically itself)**, it can **NEVER** be destroyed.

There will be more discussion about Space-Time and dimensions, but for now, let us go to the next chapter and talk about energy. (https://en.wikipedia.org/wiki/Black_hole_information_paradox   http://en.wikipedia.org/wiki/Information_paradox http://physicsworld.com/cws/article/news/2011/aug/15/information-paradox-simplified)

"If you want to find the secrets of the universe, think in terms of energy, frequency and vibrations."
-- Nikola Tesla

VI.   The Energy:

As mentioned, this theory is based on understanding (revised perception) of energy, after all, according to **Albert Einstein**, everything is created from energy, therefore mass, matter, force and energy are actually <u>**one-and-the-same**</u>. Unfortunately, if you try to find an explanation of what is energy, you'll immediately encounter descriptions such as "chemical", "atomic (nuclear)", "kinetic", "potential", and so on...

Almost all of which are descriptions of falsified human perceptions, but in no way the energy. What is (definition of) energy? To answer, let us look into powers we are using. From burning calories, fossil fuels, wood, to all other chemical reactions, nuclear fission and fusion, wind, water and electricity currents, all share several similar characteristics and one in particular. All have friction[1] (resistance), acceleration[2] (pressure/volt/speed) and volume[3] (mass/current/accelerations suspended (compressed) in Space-Time) per period of aging-time[4], but most importantly, **ALL have to be in <u>motion</u>**, following simple principle of pressure differences, where high pressure region (logical one) <u>**ACCELERATING**</u> into the low pressure region (logical zero) of similar substance or so called "vacuum". In fact, everything in our universe, from very small to very big, in constant motion and based on the wave principle (wave is another word for acceleration). I think that is precisely why **Isaac Newton** created laws of <u>**motion**</u>. (Pure motion cannot be measured in aging-time intervals as they are <u>**one-and-the-same**</u>. Please read this theory in its entirety to understand why.)

Therefore, for now, it is safe to speculate that <u>energy is two-dimensional motion-information constantly shifting into four-dimensional FORCE experienced by us as pressure and known to us as ACCELERATION.</u> <u>Motion-information is a metaphysical (two-dimensional) property and in its pure form, existed long before matter,</u> and it is because of the motion-information we exist. <u>Yes, motion can and does exist without movement of matter.</u> For example; flow of magnetic field, electrical currents, flow of gravity, flow of Space-Time, radio waves and all other forms of so called electromagnetic radiations. <u>Motion-Information is both, energy and energy conveyance</u> (the force) and that is precisely why all manifestations of acceleration are <u>squared</u> (V^2, P^2, C^2, the **inverse-square law** http://en.wikipedia.org/wiki/Inverse-square_law). (More in chapters; "The Force", "Gravity", "Electricity", "Light", "The Bridge" and "Flip-Flop Continuity"). Some, of course, would argue about potential energy, but it's true only if you are within some force. Your stretched spring will not contract if exposed to extreme cold (close to absolute zero http://en.wikipedia.org/wiki/Bose-Einstein_condensate), and ball on the shelf will not fall without gravity. Therefore, potential energy does NOT actually exist and is indication of human false perception. Where and how we got this energy? It's well known and accepted theory of the universe created from "Big-Bang" Inflation. I'm sure you heard sentence - "At first there was nothing, and then, there was everything", indicating extreme suddenty, violence, pressure and density. Therefore, motion-information is two-dimensional energy and "Big-Bang" inflation or <u>acceleration</u> (which is motion on itself) is a conveyance (the force) that created our universe. Unfortunately, some people do not understand the concept of nothing and think in terms of matter and forces associated with it. Nothing doesn't mean absence of absolutely everything, there was energy or **ACCELERATION** of the energy conveyance we perceive as inflation or shock wave (so called "bang"), however, outcomes such as gravity, magnetism, strong and weak nuclear forces did not existed (especially in forms and ways we are experiencing today). Those <u>**"forces" were created by matter**</u> and we'll talk about it later. (http://en.wikipedia.org/wiki/Energy   http://en.wikipedia.org/wiki/Force   http://en.wikipedia.org/wiki/Power_(physics)) Just remember, our entire universe is expanding and that means everything is in constant rearrangement (and only forward) within Space-Time. It also means that all those changes (as a whole) constantly creating new motion-information which is **ENERGY**. (Please refer to chapters "The Force", "Light", "The Substance", "The Big-Bang" and "Summary").

<u>It's not the fall (acceleration) that kills, but an abrupt stop!</u>

VII.   The Force:

Contrary to popular acceptance there is actually only <u>ONE</u> force!

As you most certainly aware, in classical physics there are four fundamental forces: Gravity, Electromagnetism, Strong and Weak nuclear forces. However, all those divisions on separate forces are results of falsified human perceptions. You see, in nature, there are no such things as push or pull, attraction or repulsion. Everything you do and everything you are, actually not only same energy, but also same force! Whether you are pushing or pulling, jumping or falling, breathing or even snoring, all those actions and reactions in reality are **ACCELERATIONS**. Throughout this theory you'll encounter many examples pointing to the existence of only one force, because force, at its fundamental nature, is not just an interaction of massive bodies (as it was perceived by Newton), but actually geometrical structure of two-dimensional energy, **shifted**, into four-dimensional (wave) substance and trying to shift back into its original form. As mentioned in chapter "Introduction", this theory doesn't contradict classical mechanics and Newton's second law "Force = mass multiplied by acceleration" (F=ma) is very true and useful, because in the above formula force is a mathematical calculable value and not a physical (geometrical) concept. (http://en.wikipedia.org/wiki/Newton's_laws_of_motion) But at its fundamental nature force is acceleration or pressure-wave because everything, including mass and matter, made from same substance and therefore also accelerations. (http://en.wikipedia.org/wiki/Mass_in_special_relativity) (To truly understand energy, force, mass and matter, please **study** entire theory) And if you have hard time to contemplate that you are made from energy and therefore force, then consult **Albert Einstein** and his most famous formula "Energy = mass multiplied by speed of light squared" ($E=mc^2$). As you can see, both formulas are using mass multiplied by some kind of acceleration. (Concept known as Fundamental Interaction or Interactive Force: http://en.wikipedia.org/wiki/Fundamental_interaction). As shown in previous chapter ("Energy"), the very requirement of multiplication on itself any type of so called kinetic energy (http://en.wikipedia.org/wiki/Kinetic_energy) in formulas such as Velocity (V^2) (https://en.wikipedia.org/wiki/Velocity), Momentum (P^2) (http://en.wikipedia.org/wiki/Momentum), Speed of Light (C^2) (http://en.wikipedia.org/wiki/Speed_of_light) is an indication of transitioning of mass to force and then to energy and vice-versa. If you driving car forward and come to complete **stop**, you'll experience very short and very sudden pull (a jolt) back. In electricity this effect is known as Back or Counter E.M.F. (counter-electromotive force http://en.wikipedia.org/wiki/Counter-electromotive_force). The reason, is because when you get to complete **stop**, your atoms and molecules are stopped, but the energy (mass) between, is still moving (same energy that is gets released by chemical reactions). As you know, all atoms and molecules are holding in place by magnetic interactions, so when energy is moving forward applying pressure to atoms, it changes the overall equilibrium (chaotic or self-arranged balance), the analogy would be like stretched rubber band or spring, and when it **stops**, and acquired mass converted back into Space-Time, the atoms are jumping back in-place (returning into state of chaotic balance) creating very sudden and very short wave (same reason why and how abrupt **stop** can injure or even kill). Let say you have a wet tennis ball and you want to draw-out some of the water. If you hit it against the ground as hard as you can, some of the water will be leaving the ball, because as it deforms and **stops**, the water is still moving due to inertia and momentum, same as energy (manifesting as, in form of, force) moves into and out of matter. Here we should turn to the reason why it is impossible to move throughout Space-Time faster than the speed of light. (http://en.wikipedia.org/wiki/Speed_of_light) As it stated by **Albert Einstein**, the faster you are moving the more mass you are gaining. (http://en.wikipedia.org/wiki/Special_theory_of_relativity http://en.wikipedia.org/wiki/General_relativity) That is because both Space-Time and mass, while made from same (two-dimensional) energy, in actuality, **inside universe**, flows as (**FOUR-DIMENSIONAL**) force experienced by us as pressure-waves (http://en.wikipedia.org/wiki/P-wave), or more precisely – **ACCELERATION**. Basically, energy is analog (two-dimensional) version of the substance known as motion-information and force is "digitized" or four-dimensional version of the same substance. To fully understand the concept and mechanics of conversion four-dimensional Space-Time (force) to "chemical" and "atomic" mass and vice-versa, please refer to chapters; "Gravity", "Space-Time", "Light", "The Bridge", "Flip-Flop Universe", "Dimensions & Spatial-Geometry" and "Summary". (http://en.wikipedia.org/wiki/Inverse-square_law   http://en.wikipedia.org/wiki/Unified_field_theory http://en.wikipedia.org/wiki/Quantum_electrodynamics)

http://en.wikipedia.org/wiki/GravitoElectroMagnetism

GEM equations	Maxwell's equations
$\nabla \cdot \mathbf{E}_g = -4\pi G \rho_g$	$\nabla \cdot \mathbf{E} = \dfrac{\rho}{\epsilon_0}$
$\nabla \cdot \mathbf{B}_g = 0$	$\nabla \cdot \mathbf{B} = 0$
$\nabla \times \mathbf{E}_g = -\dfrac{\partial \mathbf{B}_g}{\partial t}$	$\nabla \times \mathbf{E} = -\dfrac{\partial \mathbf{B}}{\partial t}$
$\nabla \times \mathbf{B}_g = 4\left(-\dfrac{4\pi G}{c^2}\mathbf{J}_g + \dfrac{1}{c^2}\dfrac{\partial \mathbf{E}_g}{\partial t} \right)$	$\nabla \times \mathbf{B} = \dfrac{1}{\epsilon_0 c^2}\mathbf{J} + \dfrac{1}{c^2}\dfrac{\partial \mathbf{E}}{\partial t}$
GEM equation	**EM equation**
$\mathbf{F} = m\gamma(\mathbf{v})\left(\mathbf{E}_g + \mathbf{v} \times \mathbf{B}_g \right)$	$\mathbf{F} = q\left(\mathbf{E} + \mathbf{v} \times \mathbf{B} \right)$

http://en.wikipedia.org/wiki/Eternal_inflation

Leonard Susskind, lecture on Eternal Inflation.
https://www.youtube.com/watch?v=HTCjTFZwBt4

http://en.wikipedia.org/wiki/Scalar_field_theory

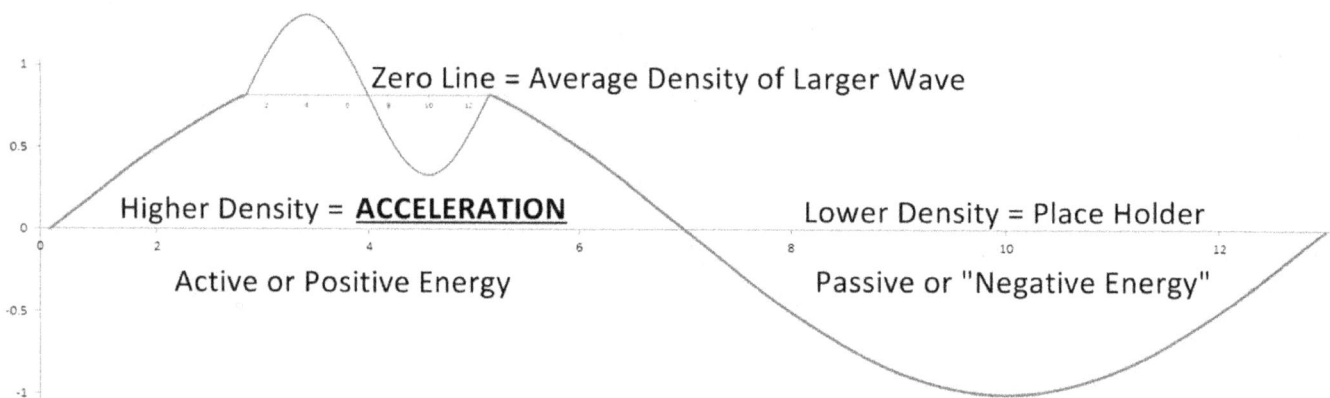

http://en.wikipedia.org/wiki/Scalar_field

Zero Line = Average Density of Larger Wave

Higher Density = **ACCELERATION**   Lower Density = Place Holder

Active or Positive Energy   Passive or "Negative Energy"

"Of course, we're all a mass of contradictions." **-- Shirley MacLaine**

VIII.   Mass & Matter:

The next obvious question, what is mass and matter, and how does energy converted into matter? Before answering let us look into some phenomenon we experience and observe in our everyday lives and also destructive forces we unleashed. First, envision a tractor-trailer speeding through the air. Because of non-aerodynamical shape it creates regions of high density of air in front and low density behind. It is very obvious why there is a high density region in front, but what makes it create a low density region behind? Well, if we could see the air, we would observe places where air **curls** on itself literally accelerating and squeezing itself into bubbles. (Effect know as turbulence.) We can also look into atomic mushroom where, debris first goes straight up and then splits and **curls** on itself. There are many examples of curling in nature, and in water we observe it as cavitation (precisely because those bubbles are spherical), but you got the idea. Our "Big-Bang" inflation was so sudden and so dense it made portions of energy (shock or pressure-wave) to **curl** on itself creating <u>bubbles</u> of energy we perceive as a subatomic particle named protons. Not only curl, but also squeezed so tight where it has no choice but to keep vibrating and curling like never ending and unpredictable hurricane reflecting (resonating) on itself. As it happened some of the energy got wrapped around protons (so called "electron" probability cloud or "atomic" energy) creating majority of the mass (concepts known as Higgs Field http://simple.wikipedia.org/wiki/Higgs_field and Higgs Boson http://en.wikipedia.org/wiki/Higgs_boson). Therefore, mass and matter are curled (squeezed) and wrapped (trapped) energy (http://en.wikipedia.org/wiki/Specific_gravity), and what we perceive as charges, actually different directions of curl. If counterclockwise (more accurately, down) curled bubbles our "normal" matter, then clockwise (more accurately, up) curled bubbles are antimatter (and vice-verse). Remember, spiral circle and full wave actually **one-and-the-same**, regardless of the state of matter. (Please read chapter "Big-Bang Inflation" for more, in-depth explanation.) There is another explanation or view of the mass. Because mass is energy manifested as force and in much higher density (saturation), aging-time inside flows at a much slower pace and length is contracted. Basically, mass is acceleration (force) outside of our "normal" Space-Time (gravity), and that is why before Einstein we didn't perceive mass as energy and force. There are also reasons to consider emergence/release of matter (hydrogen H1 http://en.wikipedia.org/wiki/Hydrogen_atom) during Supernova and Hypernova <u>implosion-explosion</u> and so called dark matter (gravity) interactions. In my opinion, only proton can be considered, more or less, as a true particle, precisely because only protons do not naturally decay **<u>within our Space-Time</u>**. All other so called "particles" have a very short lifespan and rapidly decay, including all forms of radiations (http://en.wikipedia.org/wiki/Redshift). (More in chapters "Gravity", "Electricity", "Light", "Space-Time", "Mycelium Field Universe", "Inside the Cocoon", "Dimensions & Spatial-Geometry" and "Summary")

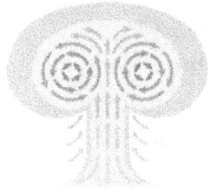

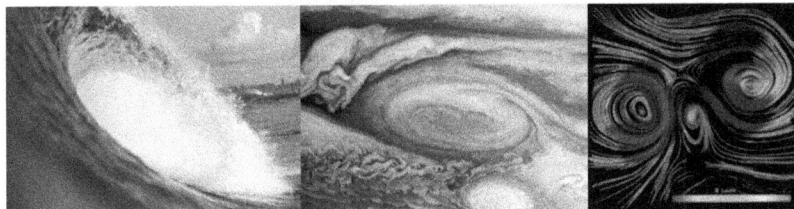

Do NOT call gravity pull (attractive) force!!!

IX. Gravity:

Before explaining gravity, I'd like to talk about acceleration (https://en.wikipedia.org/wiki/Acceleration). Many people understand acceleration as constant increase in speed; however, it's not quite accurate. Most of us driving a car, and if you are going on leveled (flat) highway, let say at 60 miles per hour and want to keep constant speed, you'll have to constantly accelerate your car (push gas pedal) because part of the energy is dissipated through various frictions and air resistance. But if road would go steeply up-heel, then your speed will decrease even if you increase acceleration to a maximum. Acceleration can be slowed-down or "stopped" completely turning it into pressure and mass (so called dark matter or gravity), an invisible cloud or halo around an object. As you know, constant acceleration due to centrifugal force or any other force(s) creates artificial gravity. As mentioned many times before (and after) perception is a major factor to understand our reality. For example; let say there is a swivel door to a kitchen, and your <u>ONLY</u> goal is to get on the other side. Obviously, door can be opened both ways (push or pull), however, from the early age you've been told that the proper way to open would be to pull. Hence, you are at the door, suddenly realizing that your hands are full and there is no handle on the door. You can simply push the door spending as little energy as needed, but your perception, forcing you to put down the bags, to free your hands, then find a way to somehow attach handle, pull the door open, hold it with your body or foot, picking up bags and proceeding into a kitchen. In the end, you've spent thousands time more energy than needed, all because of wrong perception, even though the formula to calculate gravity is the same. Consequently, is gravity attraction or **ACCELERATION**?

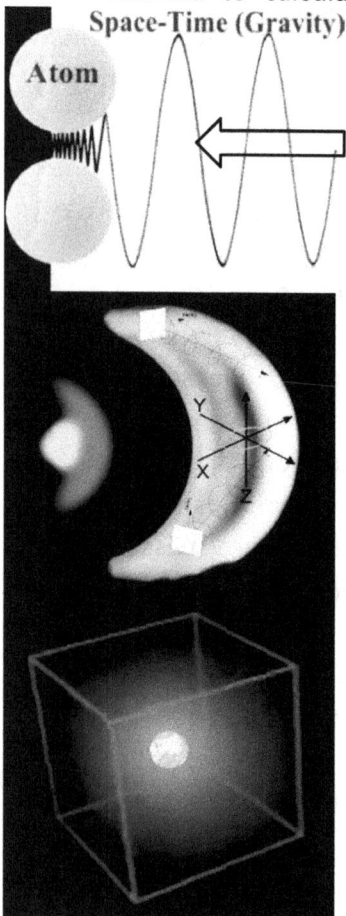

Space-Time (Gravity)

Atom

To understand gravity, let us go back to the "Big-Bang" inflation and look at the energy or motion (acceleration) of the "Bang" itself, also known as a shock wave, and on inevitable patterns of <u>wave interferences</u>. Due to inflation or stretching of the shock wave, density got lower and it evenly filled ever expanding Space-Time we perceive as our universe. Because of the wave interference, the flow of shock wave became smooth (chaotically balanced) and uniformed (directionally even). Of course, some of the energy got trapped inside atoms and as free flowing energy encountered trapped and "curled" (matter) it had no choice but to change <u>wavelength and frequency</u> (pile up around matter). Same process happened later with energy between molecules. As a result matter start's clunk (<u>accelerated</u>) into giant gas clouds we know today as the clouds (pillars) of creation. The greater atomic density or mass, the more free flowing energy is trapped (which is majority of mass in atoms) and therefore greater gravitational <u>acceleration</u>. Consequently, <u>gravity is not an attractive or pull force, but an accelerative force</u> of relatively (to free flowing energy) higher density (saturation) of Space-Time. If free flowing energy (fabric of Space-Time) like air (in terms of density) then gravity (by comparison) air (Space-Time) under gradually increasing pressure (density, saturation). You can picture it like a traffic jam where energy piled up around mass. Just like cars in traffic trickle through "bottle neck", **SUBSTANCE** of Space-Time trickles through matter. (http://en.wikipedia.org/wiki/Spacetime)

Yes, Einstein's depiction of Space-Time as fabric and gravity as curvature is somewhat suitable, however, in my opinion, more accurate (FOUR-DIMENSIONAL) explanation would be to visualize Space-Time (free flowing energy) as large cube of clear gelatin that you can see through. If we push inside some spherical object, it would displace (squeeze against substance's mass) gelatin in all directions, creating regions of higher density (ACCELERATION STRENGTH) of gelatin next to the object, where density would slowly dissipate into original saturation of gelatin, following the <u>INVERSE SQUARE LAW</u>. (http://en.wikipedia.org/wiki/Inverse-square_law)

That curving and dissipating higher density Space-Time is Gravity.

The fabric of Space-Time does have mass (dark flow, dark energy, dark matter) and that mass constantly <u>pushing **(accelerating)**</u> matter. Hence, even though majority of energy does flow through matter (WIMPs, neutrinos), heavier atoms make it flow slower (tighter "bottle neck") creating more gravity. For better understanding, let us look at water inside the space-station (or shuttle). For water to remain liquid there should be appropriate temperature and pressure. Also, gravity is needed so water can flow like we observe in nature. If we expose water to open space it would freeze and vaporize at once. But inside space-station (or shuttle) there is temperature and pressure, however, there is no gravity (to be more precise, micro-gravity) and water clunks into sphere(s) and floats. It takes the spherical form because gas <u>pushing **(accelerating)**</u> it equally from all directions (same reason why all stars and planets are spherical). Therefore, the same force (call it "dark flow", "dark energy", "dark matter", gravity, inflation, mass, force, wave, flux, pressure, acceleration, Space-Time) makes matter clunk together and move (accelerate) away from each other. (Einsteins' "Cosmological Constant") To understand how, picture two gas clouds in space. Between them several light years of Space-Time pushing (accelerating) apart, however, on all other sides there are several billion light years of Space-Time pushing (accelerating) toward each other. As mentioned above, space does have mass (acceleration), and that mass will eventually <u>accelerate</u> both clouds into one, therefore creating greater density (saturation) and as a result greater pressure inside, which in turn starts the process of creating stars and galaxies.

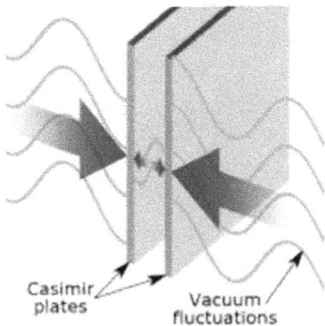

Casimir plates   Vacuum fluctuations

For example, moon does not attract water in oceans, but simply acts as an antigravity device, changing the gravitational balance of Earth. It is always all about balance and rebalance (power) of forces and matter as our entire universe is built on a simple binary system of higher region (logical one) and lower region (logical zero) saturations (density, pressure) which are perceived by us as <u>WAVES</u>. On the depiction below, you can see Space-Time between planets as inflating balloons where same force would bring planets "A" and "B" toward each other and would move planet "C" away from "B". (So called Casimir effect http://en.wikipedia.org/wiki/Casimir_effect   https://en.wikipedia.org/wiki/Cosmic_acceleration)

Therefore, gravity is collected (augmented) mass of Space-Time (so called dark matter) around and within massive objects and groups of matter (gas and dust clouds). You can view Earth like a nucleus of an atom, and gravity around would be the electron probability cloud. We all know the effects of the shock wave in cases being outside of it, but what if you are in and within the wave itself? What if you are a part of the shock wave? What if your very existence is based on certain density of the wave? As you probably guessed, all waves are pressure-waves (i.e. ACCELERATION), all waves go through the process of natural decay (mathematically know as an equation) or thinning and eventually dissipating due to inflation or stretching (the entropy), and finally, all waves are made from smaller waves, where each full wave is a 360° loop and where between zero point and pick point is always 90° when, in fact, both points are **one-and-the-same**, as both are an indication of flip (<u>**stop**</u>) points. Are you confused yet? I know I am. And unless we stop relying so heavily on our, human, perceptions (measuring everything in terms of Space-Time) and "rewire" our brain, to include possibility being at once everywhere and nowhere-in-particular, the true nature of our physical world would keep eluding us.

(More in chapter "Quantum Theory"   http://en.wikipedia.org/wiki/Cosmological_constant)

(http://en.wikipedia.org/wiki/Gravitational_lens http://en.wikipedia.org/wiki/Supergravity https://www.youtube.com/watch?v=jremlZvNDuk)

"I could trust a fact and always cross-question an assertion." **-- Michael Faraday**

X.   Magnetism:

Finally, we got to the "force" which is most obvious and easiest to test and prove.

What is (definition of) magnetism? We, obviously, know how magnetic field forms, and why there is always "North Pole" and "South Pole". But why there is always 90° inclination? Why everything interacts with it? Why all elementary particles, such as light (photons), heat, x-ray, other so called electromagnetic radiations and radio waves derivatives of magnetism and can also interact with all fundamental forces? If we examine any magnetic field, we can see that on both polls field looks like a funnel. In fact, there is such thing in nature which is known as **funnel effect**, and we can observe this in twisters, vortexes, black holes, atomic mushrooms. For a demonstration, I'll get a glass of water and if I spin something in it, we'll observe the funnel effect and there will always be 90° inclination between spinning object (orbital inclination) and funnel (magnetic pole). We already discussed how apple resembles magnetic field, and as you can see on the picture below, same is true for pilled orange. There are other objects in nature that are more or less resemble magnetic field, precisely because everything is made from the same energy and as a result must follow same set of physical (geometrical) structures. (http://classes.yale.edu/fractals/   http://www.amazon.com/Fractal-Geometry-Mathematical-Foundations-Applications/dp/0470848626)

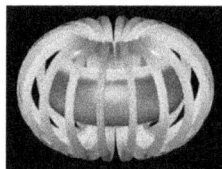

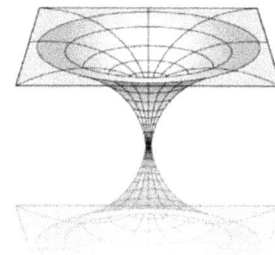

Why we do not observe in <u>tor</u>nados and vortexes fully developed <u>tor</u>us, looking like magnetic field? That is because gases and liquids do not spin with speed of light, can exist only within Space-Time and therefore never experience energy vacuums, plus there is also a matter of viscosity. The energy, on the other hand, does move at the speed of light, doesn't have viscosity, and as it accelerates up and away by the centrifugal force to the "north pole", energy encounters vacuum (lack of acceleration) at the "south pole". As you know, vacuum doesn't suck (attracts) anything, but energy, as well as matter, always wants to accelerate into a vacuum, in order to equalize pressure (balance it out), and the closest source of the energy is the one that is accelerated to the "north pole", so energy bands and completes geometrical form we know as torus. (http://en.wikipedia.org/wiki/Torus) Therefore magnetism – is trapped free flowing energy, between the nucleus and orbital inclinations of what's known to us as "electrons" (so called "electron" probability cloud), being spanned by spinning proton (atomic nucleus) creating funnel effects due to centrifugal force. There is one crucial difference; energy, unlike matter, does not have viscosity (as viscosity is magnetic interaction between atoms and molecules) and because trapped energy spinning with speeds close to the speed of light, magnetic field behaves different from funnel effects we observe in air and water. As far as charges, there is no such thing. The direction of the particle spin creates an impression of charge. In reality it's a simple difference of <u>energy density</u> give us positive (low or negative density also known as holes) and negative (high or positive density perceived as free "electrons") charges.

(http://en.wikipedia.org/wiki/Eddy_current   http://en.wikipedia.org/wiki/Electron   http://en.wikipedia.org/wiki/Gamma_ray)

XI.   Electricity:

It is accepted and unfortunately not very accurate (completed) explanation of free "electrons" moving thru material. In reality, electricity is a directional (pulsating) or bidirectional (oscillating) movement (or gradual changes in density also known as <u>waves</u>) of trapped energy (known as flux, cold plasma or "electron" probability cloud) created by manipulation of orbital inclinations and, as a result, angular momentum and angular velocity (http://en.wikipedia.org/wiki/Angular_momentum http://en.wikipedia.org/wiki/Angular_velocity) (centrifugal force http://en.wikipedia.org/wiki/Centrifugal_force). It is in fact pulsating current created by high to low propagation of energy (waves). In order to understand electricity we must first understand electrically conductive materials and their natural state. If you visualize wire made out of particles, it would look somewhat like the corn on a husk ("electron" probability clouds). All those atomic nuclei are held in

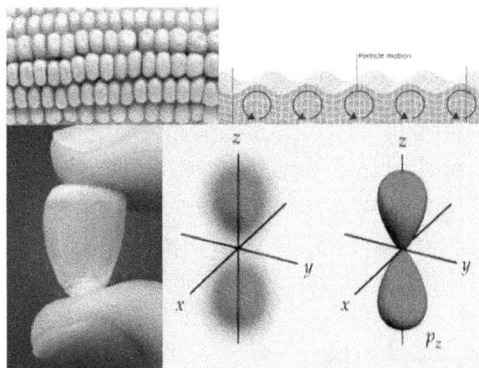

place by the magnetic fields interactions around them. The wire itself, what's known in quantum mechanics, is a collection of so called "standing" waves, basically "frozen" (compressed) in Space-Time. Majority of matter, around us, is in constant state of chaotically arranged (balanced) configuration, meaning that magnetic tori around the atom nuclei, arranged so both "north" and "south" poles equally and spherically directed (or balanced) with all other tori around it. (Spherical harmonics https://en.wikipedia.org/wiki/Spherical_harmonics) The spin of the atomic nucleus creates centrifugal forces, that force is manifested as magnetic fields, where the poles of neighboring atoms arranging themselves into magnetic equilibrium (chaotically balanced). By moving stronger magnetic field near wire, we are changing orbital inclinations and therefore angular momentum and angular velocity of the orbitals as poles aligning with stronger magnetic field, thus creating regions of higher density on the one site of the atom (perceived as negative charge or free "electrons") and lower density on the other (perceived as positive charge or holes). Of course, the atoms located further away from surface area are less affected or un-affected at all, that is why most of the electricity in wires flows closest to the surface (lower resistance). To better understand, let us go back to our tractor-trailer speeding though air and look at regions of higher and lower density. If we flatten tractor-trailer and place several of them one behind another, the higher density flux would accelerate into lower region, creating waves or domino effect (http://en.wikipedia.org/wiki/Domino_effect http://en.wikipedia.org/wiki/Quantum_tunnelling), trying to equalize and return back into chaotically (self-arranged) balanced state. Therefore we can also consider all atoms of the wire as batteries connected in series and parallel where wave flowing (pulsating) in one direction as direct current or oscillate as alternating current. Just picture, orbital cloud rings, spinning around nucleus and as outside magnetic field passes, the atomic magnetic field ("electron" probability clouds) aligning itself changing inclination. The circumference remains the same, but orientation of angular velocity, changes and as stronger magnetic field is moving away, orbitals returning to their original inclinations, as they interact with other (deeper) fields, and at much faster pace. This phenomenon of orbitals returning to their original inclinations, known as "kick back", spike, Back or Counter E.M.F. (counter-electromotive force http://en.wikipedia.org/wiki/Counter-electromotive_force), and occurs whenever we switch lights ON or OFF (refer to chapter "The Force"). The analogy would be slow stretched spring suddenly tightening, creating in the process much higher acceleration (voltage). Remember, compared to the speed of light, passing objects are moving at very slow motions. Whenever we produce electricity we are quite literally pumping **FORCE** (cold plasma) inside the wire like water inside the hose. Yes, it is possible to use electricity to produce (convert gravity into) much more electricity. And NO, it's not a "Perpetual Mobile" as nothing in this universe, and even the universe itself, is forever.

(More in chapters "Light", "The Bridge", "Dimensions & Spatial-Geometry", "Summary" & "Appendix A")

"It is during our darkest moments that we <u>must focus</u> to see the light." -- Aristotle Onassis

XII.   Light:

If you remember chapters "Waves" and "Motion-Information" you should know, that everything in our universe, including Space-Time itself, travels in conically shaped (inflating) spiral motions we perceive as waves. You should also remember that Space-Time is a **four-dimensional substance** and just like any substance varies in density also known as saturation, pressure or more precisely **acceleration strength**. Why is it so important for us to realize this perception of Space-Time and perceive it as virtual spirals? That is because light and other "electro-magnetic" radiations do not actually travel anywhere the way we would expect particles and matter travel throughout Space-Time.

To understand how light **PROPAGATES** throughout Space-Time we should look into phenomenon known as a domino effect (http://en.wikipedia.org/wiki/Quantum_tunnelling). Just like dominos falling and pushing each other, so called electro-magnetic radiations vibrate Space-Time itself and that vibration is propagating throughout each coil of our virtual conical spirals of the Space-Time. That is why light propagation speed directly correlates to the density of the Space-Time and creates an illusion of unchangeable speed of light and actual length contraction, where if you accelerate throughout Space-Time with increasing speed, the speed of light remains the same, and Space-Time flows at slower rate. Concepts known as time dilation and length contraction (http://en.wikipedia.org/wiki/Time_dilation http://en.wikipedia.org/wiki/Length_contraction). If you accept this kind of reasoning then you should also realize that colors are NOT wavelength of light (as we experience), but actually a saturation differences of Space-Time (known as plasma, flux or "electron" probability cloud) inside minerals and gases. Please remember, **SPACE IS TIME AND TIME IS SPACE!** There is no crisscrossing as often depicted in explanations of "fabric" of Space-Time. That depiction is two-axial and messes with our perception. In general, light has only one color, white, and all other colors are indications of certain Space-Time saturations, meaning aging-time is actually flows at different rates and we receiving **information**, of those paces, in forms of so called electromagnetic radiations and identifying them as colors (red<u>shift</u> effect https://en.wikipedia.org/wiki/Redshift   http://en.wikipedia.org/wiki/Tired_light).

Furthermore, all colors (including white and black) are illusions created by our brains and perceived by our minds in response to some Space-Time vibrations (vibrational saturation) or lack of such.

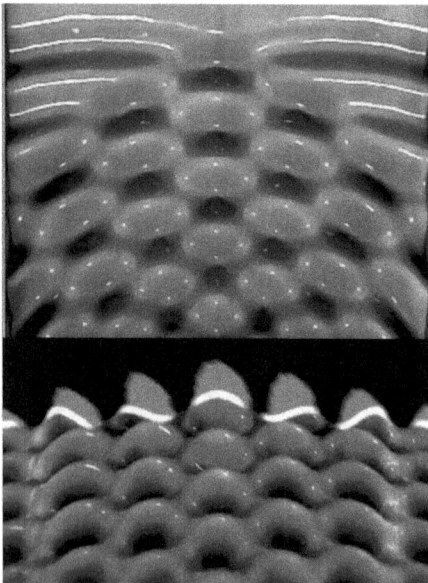

<u>Observe the wave interference patterns on the pictures of double slit experiment. As you see, the propagation of high and low regions, occurring not only up-down, but also left-right and in a circular pattern. Turn on your imagination and try to see it not in two-axis, as it shown, but like under water in four-dimensions, and you'll see those shapes as large inflating balloons made-up by inflating balloons breaking on smaller inflating balloons (bubbles or spheres known as cavitation), structured like spiral strings. Each full wave is SPHERICAL IN SHAPE (geometry) and SPIRAL IN STRUCTURE (motion), where high saturation region looks like a membrane of the bubble and low saturation region, its cavity</u>. *(This is why caverning electrons are considered negatively charged.)* Most of us perceive structure as something rigid, like a building, bridge and so on…, but as those structures formed, they are literally grow in size (mass) and, without constant maintenance, will deteriorate, finally reducing back to dust. Therefore structures are ongoing arrangements of geometrical propagations. As you can see, we keep getting back to the waves, because everything made of waves and "wave" (force or pressure) is another word for **ACCELERATION**.

You can repeat double slit experiment with white smoke; however, to see inside the large inflating sphere and observe smaller ones, you would have to shine bright light. Just as scientists have to shine laser to penetrate "electron probability" cloud. (https://www.youtube.com/watch?v=qqSyQNv8DmY) Let say there are two cameras recording events at crisscrossing angles, where light traveling from recorded objects to each camera has to cross, as shown on the picture below. (http://en.wikipedia.org/wiki/Atomic_orbital)

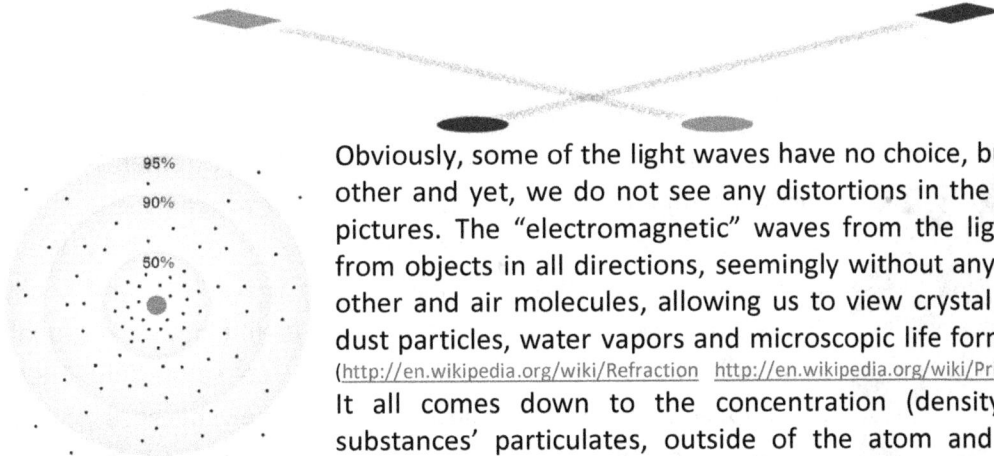

Obviously, some of the light waves have no choice, but to interact with each-other and yet, we do not see any distortions in the quality of the recorded pictures. The "electromagnetic" waves from the light source are bouncing from objects in all directions, seemingly without any interactions with each-other and air molecules, allowing us to view crystal clear images even with dust particles, water vapors and microscopic life forms suspended in the air. (http://en.wikipedia.org/wiki/Refraction http://en.wikipedia.org/wiki/Prism)

It all comes down to the concentration (density, saturation) of given substances' particulates, outside of the atom and around atomic nuclei. We have many names for the actual substance surrounding each nucleus. Probability cloud, magnetic flux, cold plasma, mass, Space-Time, pressure-waves, acceleration and more… Yes, it is strange to consider mass and force as being same substance, but I would like to remind, that word substance came from word substantial and those two values are interchangeable. For example: if you have one hundred watt bulb, you can power it by applying hundred volts and one amp, or you can apply ten volts and ten amps, or one thousand volts and hundred milliamps… As you can see on the image above, the "probability" cloud is made up of the waves created by nucleus spin, where regions most probable of detecting "electrons" are the highest in saturation. As for the prism experiment, the reason we observe distinct (rainbow) colors and not the smooth (blurred) transitioning, is because passing light, mostly interacts with higher saturated or crest regions of the clouds' full waves.

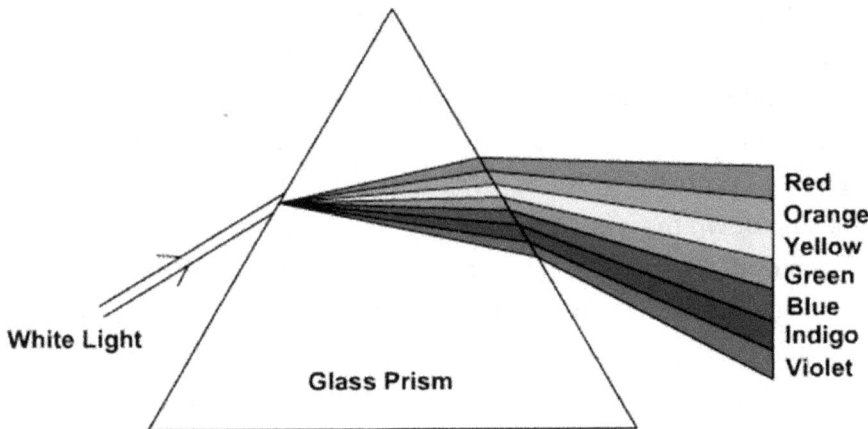

http://en.wikipedia.org/wiki/Grand_Unified_Theory
http://en.wikipedia.org/wiki/Theory_of_everything
http://en.wikipedia.org/wiki/String_theory
http://en.wikipedia.org/wiki/M-theory

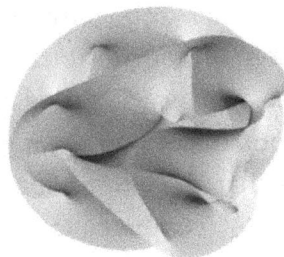

"There is nothing in the world except empty curved space. Matter, charge, electromagnetism, and other fields are only manifestations of the curvature of space." **-- John Wheeler**

XIII.   Space-Time:

First of all, it is NEVER just space and/or just time! You can **NEVER** move in spatial-geometry without moving by the same amount in aging-time and vice-versa. (http://en.wikipedia.org/wiki/Spacetime) **SPACE IS TIME AND TIME IS SPACE!** If you think you are moving only in aging-time while sitting in your room or sleeping in your bed, then you MUST remember that Earth is spinning on its axis and also moving around the Sun and our solar system revolving around center of our "Milky Way" galaxy and entire galaxy is flying through Space-Time and finally Space-Time itself is expanding (stretching in all three-axial spatial-geometry, thus thinning in terms of density, i.e. saturation). There are two ways to explain Space-Time, precisely because of our, human, perception. First, let us talk about passage of aging-time the way we experience. Contrary to popular believe, length of life is not based on seconds, hours or years. Those are just <u>scales</u> we invented to cope with reality. The actual passage of aging-time is based on the rate of natural decay (also known as weak nuclear force); however, the decay rate itself is determined by the density (saturation) of Space-Time. The higher saturation of Space-Time (gravity, "probability clouds") will slow down the decay rate, thus slowing down the passage of aging-time. Time is also the amounts of acceleration loops passed through in one unit of continuity (for example length of your life or life of a mosquito or solar system). We all experienced moments which lasted fraction of the second, and yet, it seemed like it was a lot longer. In fact, in that particular moment, **for your mind**, aging-time actually did slow down because in that fraction of your existence you've been able to pass (use) more of the free flowing energy. Remember, energy is motion-information (waves of shifts), and not calories or particles or reactions. Those are, just like force, products of energy. The faster you move (including motion of neurons in your brain) the slower flow of aging-time. To understand how Space-Time, force and energy could be **ONE-AND-THE-SAME**, we must look into world of extremely small, known as "quantum mechanics". As we divide Space-Time trying to calculate tiny "particles" and distances they travel inside the atom, both getting so small where we no longer can distinguish one from another, because both flow in unison without distinction. In chapter "Waves" we talked about three-axial wave looking like an inflating "balloon" or "bubble". Let us look closer into the membrane of the "bubble". No matter how thin that membrane looks to us, we know it has depth, and as "bubble" continues to inflate, the membrane itself has no choice

but to stretch in all directions. Of course I'm talking about the "Big-Bang" inflation shock wave. As our virtual membrane stretching and expanding, carving spatial-geometry, it is also getting less saturated, creating aging-time as we know it. To the outside observer those processes would be apparent and trivial, but for someone who is inside that membrane and made from the same substance, being part of the "membrane" itself, the process of stretching and thinning will look somewhat confusing. If it would be easier for you to understand, you can perceive Space-Time as cold (I should say extremely cold) and stretched plasma or flux. As you know, there are **FOUR** states of matter, solid, liquid, gas and finally plasma, also known as dark matter, dark energy, gravity, aether, mass, pressure, waves, acceleration and more... Let us take units which are billion-trillion times smaller than picosecond and micron (the unit has no direct correlation to Space-Time) and call it "continuity" (mathematically always equal to one http://en.wikipedia.org/wiki/Planck_scale   http://en.wikipedia.org/wiki/Planck_time). Just for the sake of argument, suppose on one hand we have one hundred of those units and it equals to a picosecond or micron, and on another hand we have a thousand of same units but it also equals to a picosecond or micron. But how is that possible? Well, if we accept that energy is motion-information, we'll observe less motions (bigger "bubbles") (quantum fluctuations http://en.wikipedia.org/wiki/Quantum_fluctuation) per unit where we have

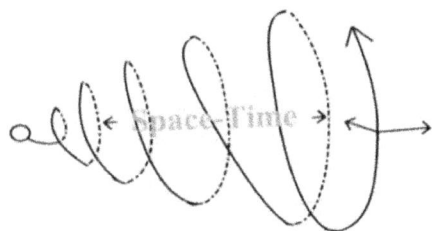

one hundred, and more motions (smaller "bubbles") per unit where we have a thousand. Therefore one flows slower and the other faster, but both are equal to one picosecond or micron. Yes, this is very confusing subject and to better understand it we must understand why lever works, why circular movement differs (has advantages) over linear in general, why and how aging-time slows down with speed and/or gravity and how time dilation works. (http://en.wikipedia.org/wiki/Time_dilation http://en.wikipedia.org/wiki/Gravitational_time_dilation)
In simplistic terms, space-time can be squeezed (increasing saturation, pressure, acceleration, slowing-down time and decreasing length) and stretched (decreasing saturation, pressure, acceleration, speeding-up time and increasing length). Those changes are governing the rate of natural decay, and that is what and how aging-time actually ticks. As you remember from chapter "Motion-Information", everything, including Space-Time, flows in virtual conical logarithmic spirals, as you can observe on the above picture, where Space-Time, in the depiction, would be distance between coiling loops. At present, the most accurate time keeping device is an Atomic Clock where the passage of time is calculated based on natural decay vibrations. We can also perceive density of Space-Time as quantum fluctuation rates. (http://en.wikipedia.org/wiki/Quantum_fluctuation)

Please remember, we are discussing passage (saturation) of Space-Time and not the length of (human or otherwise) life. (http://en.wikipedia.org/wiki/Atomic_clock   https://www.youtube.com/watch?v=bqlUNGb_aQ4)
(More in chapter "Inside the Cocoon")

"If we knew what we were doing, it wouldn't be called research, would it?" **-- Albert Einstein**

XIV.   The "Bridge":

As of today, there are two mathematically competing theories known to us as "Einstein's Relativity Theory" (also can be viewed as "Classical Mechanics") and "Quantum Mechanics" also known as "Probability Theory". Both theories are mathematically considered to be very accurate in calculating and predicting physical events. The purpose of this theory is to show how both laws are equally applicable to our large, classical mechanics world, and similarly true for the world of quantum mechanics.

First of all, let me point out, that both are using word "mechanics" which is another word for motion. Yes, it is very tempting to call everything counterintuitive weird and unusual just because our, human, perception is lying to us, but we, humans, have the ability to rationalize events and discard perceptions. For example, in order to detect "particles" we must shine light. But what if there are no such thing as particles and what we observe is an interaction of light waves and energy waves orbiting nucleus (so called "electron" probability cloud), just like you see on the picture. Such interaction of waves would create an appearance of particles. However, there is a bridge between both worlds and we use it every day without giving a second thought. I'm, of course, referring to the electricity or more precisely to the way we are making electricity. If you remember chapters "Motion-Information", "Magnetism" and "Electricity", you should know that all motions are circular in nature and the very act of creating electricity involves a spin. We are literary transferring "classical mechanics" spin into "quantum mechanics" spin. I would like to point out that word mechanics is another word (synonym) for word motion. Every circle, regardless of circumference, can be broken into four basic strokes, stroke one: zero to positive pick, stroke two: positive pick to zero, stroke three: zero to negative pick, and stroke four: negative pick to zero, completing full wave. In the circle each stroke is a quarter turn or 90°. The same is true for a pendulum as all motions are circular in nature. I'm intentionally trying to stay away from mathematics and formulas, however, here is the equation which is weird and counter intuitive, but nevertheless is true: "Zero Equals Infinity", as both points are **one-and-the-same** indicating transformation. $(0) \equiv \infty$

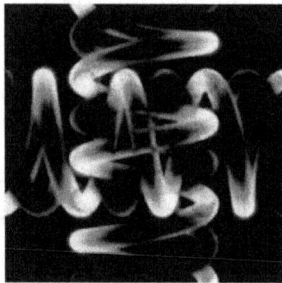

It is hard to understand and accept, but infinitely small and infinitely large are actually **one-and-the-same**. It is another closed loop and the reason why and how **information is everywhere and nowhere-in-particular**. If you familiar with electricity and assume that primary of the electrical transformer is inducing electricity on the secondary, you are both right and completely wrong, as all transformers actually **GENERATING** electricity exactly like mechanical generators producing electrical charges. Both are based on the principle involving gradual changes of the magnetic field strength, thus inducing quantum waves (spins) within electrically conductive materials. The point I'm trying to make, is that Motion-Information exists as a two-dimensional physical or more precisely metaphysical entity (substance) which is equally applicable to both classical and quantum theories without contradicting each other, therefore combining them into one "Unified Theory of <u>Most</u> Everything".

In chapter "Quantum Theory" we'll discuss the "double slit experiment", "quantum entanglement" and "quantum bit status" from the revised perceptions, but to truly understand those possibilities you should study in greater details chapters "Dimensions & Spatial-Geometry" and "Summary".

XV.   Strong & Weak Nuclear Forces:

The strong nuclear force is "created" by subatomic particles like protons and there is a great possibility that neutrons are simply curled parts of the above force. You can view strong nuclear force as gravity (on steroids) taken into extreme. To understand how, we must understand particle behavior.

As each proton escaped so called "primordial soup" it makes four distinct motions. First, it's flying away from the center of "Big-Bang" inflation, second, it's spinning or curling, third, it vibrates (as vibrating string of energy curling on itself) and finally, it wobbles. The reason it wobbles is because as it curling and vibrating, it collecting around itself free flowing energy (the substance of Space-Time) and mass of that energy (cloud) makes proton wobble. That collected energy is electron probability cloud, and will also act as strong nuclear force holding subatomic "particles" together. On the picture you see two circles with arrows, where both indicating clockwise spin direction. As shown, the arrows are pointing to each-other, meaning, the "linear" path of each cloud is on the collision trajectory. As those "extended" protons bumped to each other, some of the collected energy is looped in the opposite direction (due to clouds "head-on collisions") creating an appearance of the subatomic "particle" we call neutron. It's looping on itself and spinning in opposite direction around proton within collected energy like the hurricane eye on planet Jupiter. Those opposite directions of spin make both stay together (because of vibrations the spins would be better described as up-down and not clockwise-counterclockwise). Due to angular momentum and angular velocity (centrifugal force), energy strains (clouds) around particles move (waving) at different speeds (frequency) and on distinctive orbits, and due to constant external bombardment by "electromagnetic" radiations and also constant drop of Space-Time in saturation (pressure) strength, due to inflation, creating very short lived loops. In fact, "electrons" and other elementary particles do not actually exist as classical particles, like protons, and what we perceive as particles are only the wave interactions (so called "standing" waves). It's tightening (implosion) of the loop, creating outward waves, we perceive as natural decay radiation also known as weak nuclear force. The third Newtonian law at work; ***"For every action, there is an equal and opposite reaction"***. The tightening of the loop makes energy to shift (wave) away from the loop, like radio waves from the transmitter. It would seem like I'm giving you two unrelated explanations for the "weak nuclear force" (natural decay), but in fact it is all **one-and-the-same**, as all we are talking is about outside pressure (acceleration), whether that pressure created by something substantial as "electromagnetic" radiations, or by something seemingly insignificant as Space-Time (gravity). Both are manifestations of the Newtonian law of actions and reactions, where action-reaction pair itself is an indication of the original shifts of energy (motion-information) from two-dimensional semi-coherence into four-dimensional geometrically shaped and thus spirally structured Space-Time. And the entire "zoo" of "particles" (http://en.wikipedia.org/wiki/Standard_Model), observed in colliders (http://en.wikipedia.org/wiki/Large_Hadron_Collider), are nothing more than extremely ultra-high and therefore <u>exceedingly short lived</u> frequencies produced by head-on collisions, whether those collisions are man-made or natural.

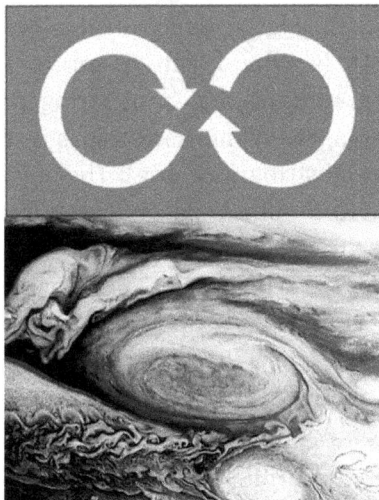

XVI.   Flip-Flop Continuity:

Starting with this chapter we'll play a mental movie, recreating steps it took to transform (shift) motion-information into Space-Time our universe, or more precisely the multiverse, is made and so are we. It all started with two-dimensional (metaphysical) entity we know today as motion-information. This entity didn't have concepts of Space-Time, because such substance did not existed. **Meaning, not only it couldn't move in Space-Time or lacked depth, but even concepts of left-right or up-down were unknown as they are simply did not existed**. The only possible motion was to change the status, flip from low to high saturation, and flop back to low…

The yin-yang effect (http://en.wikipedia.org/wiki/Yin_and_yang), which in itself is both, motion and information, and that is why I call it motion-information. You can also view it as a two-dimensional bent string of energy trying, like a dog, to catch its own tail, but remember this is just an interface and in reality there was no actual string (nor dog). There is, of course, a major advantage, being two-dimensional and lacking concepts of Space-Time and forces such as gravity, magnetism and even temperature, because two-dimensional entity is everywhere and nowhere-in-particular. As mentioned before, motion-information is ever present and accessible by anyone, anywhere at any Space-Time and in any amounts. This continued for eons without any major changes, however, every flip of status would speed up the next flop by an insignificant amount, slowly creating doubling effects known today as resonance (or constructive waves http://en.wikipedia.org/wiki/Interference_(wave_propagation)) and harmonics. And if you think speed of light is fastest in the universe, just picture yourself jumping from galaxy to galaxy or even from one universe to another. Our, thoughts have no boundaries of speed and/or Space-Time, precisely because information is everywhere and nowhere-in-particular. But nothing is forever, and even at super slow flip-flops of continuity, the resonance eventually would speed up the process of changing, waving or "spinning" so much where newly created centrifugal force would allow possibility not only to "catch its own tail", but actually overtake it (formation of so called "standing" waves), thus creating useful energy (the force) and "carving" our four-dimensional Space-Time. I would call this process a virtual shift or "vShift" (http://en.wikipedia.org/wiki/Lamb_shift). One thing we have to remember, this "vShift" did not happen at one point as there were no such things as points. If you write computer programs, especially in assembler, you would be familiar with such term as shifts. We use to think in directional shifts, shift right, shift left, but in reality all shifts occur in both directions at once. As you shift to the right, something always shifting to the left and vice-versa… For example; if you have several people standing in line, shoulder to shoulder, shifting one by one to the right, you'll observe as an "empty" spacing would shift to the left and vice-versa…, and that is where "root" for the third Newtonian law of action and reaction pair takes place. The quantum mechanics is based on shifts, which is prime indication of binary, where binary is based on ONE, having two logical states, and TWO, creating FOUR places (dimensions), where FOUR, is a primary computer word or byte. In chapter "Motion-Information" I asked you to keep in mind number FOUR as it is literary permeates our entire existence. FOUR motions of the protons (as protons escaped so called primordial soup it makes FOUR distinct motions. One; flying away from the center of a "Big-Bang", two; spinning or curling, three; vibrating (as vibrating string of energy curling on itself) and FOUR; wobbles due to acquired mass). FOUR states of matter, FOUR-dimensions, FOUR stroke engines, FOUR fundamental forces, FOUR limbs (mammals, birds, reptilians), FOUR basic rules of business, FOUR DNA organic bases (http://en.wikipedia.org/wiki/DNA) and more… There will be detailed explanation in chapter "Dimensions & Spatial-Geometry" about meaning of number FOUR. (More on two-dimensions in chapter "Summary" http://en.wikipedia.org/wiki/Ouroboros)

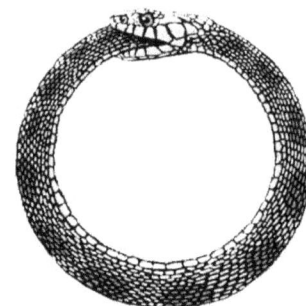

XVII.   The Substance:

In this chapter, we'll look into theory of energy substance. This depiction of concepts known as "Higgs Field" (http://simple.wikipedia.org/wiki/Higgs_field   http://en.wikipedia.org/wiki/Higgs_mechanism), String Theory and "M-Theory" (http://en.wikipedia.org/wiki/M-theory) are not classical ones and intended to explain emergence of the substance itself (the multitude of "standing" waves) and to show how and why it would lead to the "Big-Bang" Inflation. More math: 0.0∞1% where ∞ = 0. Suppose there was a wave, as shown on figure 1. To understand how stretched this wave, let say that every subatomic element of the figure 1 as large as hundreds of billions universes. Because it's so stretched its saturation almost non-existent. If you wish to go from point "A" to point "B", you have no choice but to follow entire wave. However, if portion of the wave reflected itself and would wave at crisscross pattern, creating matrix, as shown on figure 2, then it would be possible to zigzag and avoid long trip, just like you see in figure 3. But as you can see on the image, the zigzag itself is also a wave (wave of waves). And, of course, if our original wave would continue crossing in all directions, then it would appear you can connect two points with a straight line like on the last figure. But in reality we know, there are no straight lines and everything travels in waves. This is how we got the substance of energy (the field), floating very slowly and majestically in all directions at once. At this point of continuity, there were no particles, no known forces, no temperature and not even Space-Time as we know it. According to mathematics, zero multiplied, added, divided or subtracted would always produce only zero. Therefore, if our substance or field of energy never interacted with itself, there would be no universe and no us. However, if interaction rate would be as low as 0.0∞1% (precisely because field continuously expanding) then, eventually, there is a possibility for something very interesting to occur. Just as with any wave, including radio waves, interaction makes them to change frequency and wavelength creating higher density and therefore increasing probabilities for higher rate of interactions. At some point, purely by chance, the rate of interactions got spherical shape, thus creating scenario of reflecting energy inside, where interaction rate slowly starts getting higher and higher. This is a virtual sphere and there are no visible or measurable edges, and it's larger than billions of universes, but it is a sphere. As we travel deeper into our virtual sphere, we would observe smaller sphere where percent of interactions high enough to resemble faint gravitational force and if we would continue our journey, there would be region where "gravity" would be equal to 1G. The deeper we go the higher and stronger interaction rate, so much so parts of the waves would loop and as loop would tightened it would first send out waves similar to radio waves, then (as we go deeper) infrared (temperature), then light and other radiations... Soon we'll get to a sphere where field density so high it would resemble stupendously hot liquid but without viscosity. At this point we would be not far from the core and substance densities like heavy molten metal where more and more loops, sending out radiations thus creating "push-out" acceleration we perceive as weak nuclear force (Newtonian law of actions and reactions). And soon, this push out would build up so much, it would overcome all the mass of waves reflecting inside, and at this very moment our universe would inflate like a ginormous radio beacon sending out waves after waves of energy and some of those loops, creating in process more loops, but more importantly tightening some of them so much, where they have no choice but to keep curling onto themselves, thus creating seeds of matter we know as protons. (Refer to chapter "Mass & Matter")

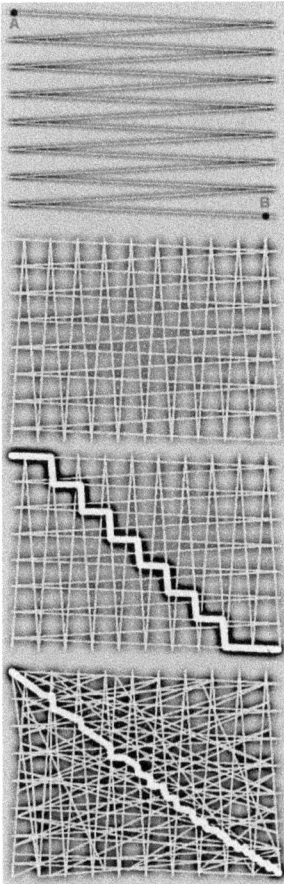

XVIII. "Big-Bang" Inflation:

To understand "Big-Bang" let us envision light reflected of parabolic mirror. At some point we will observe it, squeezing into tiny hot and bright spot and then flipping and dissipating at same angle as it was reflected. For now, let us look at the part on the dissipating site of the cross point and at some distance from it picture tiny circle (inside dissipating beam). That circle is a representation of our **observable** universe (we cannot see beyond because light and other particles and even substance of Space-Time itself do not have speed to catch-up due to inflation).

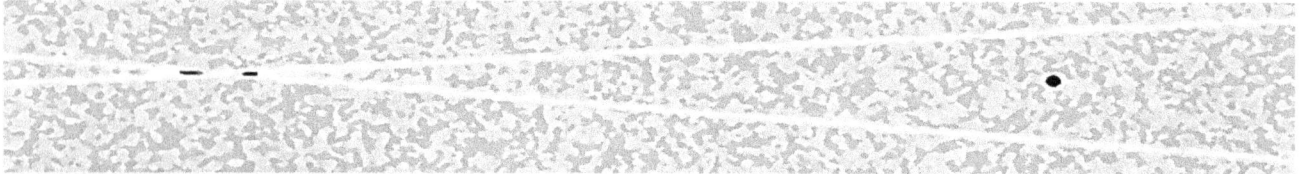

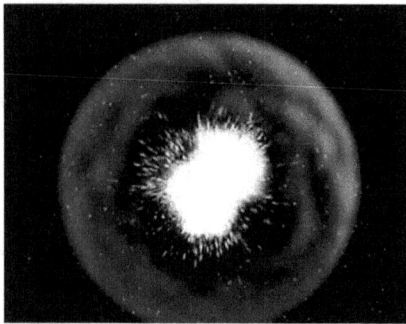

In exceedingly distant history, two-dimensional energy reflected itself from all directions into tiny spot, collected there, and then dissipated (inflated) in all directions with much greater force (pressure, acceleration), changing frequency of the flow and creating in process our universe and matter. In a sense "Big-Bang" inflation is a beacon of waves, similar to antenna transmitting radio waves. I am great proponent of the theory of "Big Rip" (http://en.wikipedia.org/wiki/Big_Rip http://www.youtube.com/watch?v=JaImVFRpOR8), therefore at some point as our universe expends and fabric of Space-Time will no longer be able to keep same density (pressure) it will reap matter to compensate, as a result there will be enormous release of energy which will cause "universe" to bend like magnetic field bends from north to south and flow back to the center of the "emergence". I trust this process is happening now and that is how energy reusing (recycling) itself over and over again. In sense, "Big-Bang" both never stopped and "never" started. As mentioned in chapter "Perception" contradiction and simplicity are the keys to understand our reality. (More in next chapter)

❖ Centrifugal and Centripetal "Forces":

By now you should know that our universe is created from substance we call "Energy", and that energy is in geometrical form we recognize as "Force". You should also remember that this "formatted" substance, due to massive pressure (acceleration) created by "Big-Bang", can and does self-pack into higher density inside matter via interactions. Furthermore, that density can be changed by speed and/or gravity, and all motions are spiral in nature. Obviously, we must not forget about ever-present actions and reactions. Why centrifugal and centripetal "forces" are there in the first place? That is because as matter moves throughout Space-Time it squeezes like a coiled spring, and just like coiled spring it creates' recoiled (reversed) linear (longitudinal) pressure. In case of the spin, Space-Time is squeezed throughout entire surface of the spinning object, but then you have more recoiled "springs" pushing on each-other from center to the edge of spinning object, creating centrifugal action and centripetal reaction. If you ever studied Tesla technologies, you'll come across his patented pump which is using this method ("phenomenon") to provide a very efficient way to pump liquids.

XIX.   "White-Hole" & "Black-Holes":

First of all, "Black-Holes" do not connect to a "White-Hole" and have absolutely nothing to do with wormholes and other intriguing theories. If you paid attention, you'll notice that this chapter calls "White-Hole" (singular) and "Black-Holes" (plural). That is because the "White-Holes" are creators of universes known to us as "Big-Bang" or Inflation, and there can be only one per universe, and "Black-Holes" are creators of galaxies and "White-Hole" wannabes. Every "Black-Hole", in theory, can grow into "White-Hole" if it "consumes" enough matter. It all comes down to the diameter of the "Black-Hole" or more precisely to the total surface area of the sphere. Just as with most physical processes, it is not always what it appears to be and our human perception standing on the way to see what it is in reality. I'd like to point out on the importance of surface area not only in "Black-Holes" but also in electricity, chemistry, biology and many other aspects of our reality. (More in chapters "Dimensions" & "Summary") In chapters "The Substance" and "Big-Bang Inflation" we talked about how energy came for the "first time" into super massive "White-Hole" and then inflated into the universe. With "Black-Hole" turning into "White-Hole" the process is a bit more complex because it already part of the inflation process, but the principle is the same. By acquiring enough matter (mass to energy) the "Black-Hole" can grow to such humongous size where total surface area would overwhelm "weak-force" at which point it would no longer needed matter to enlarge and starts slowly grow even bigger just by compressing (consuming) Space-Time. The above process, of course, very speculative because in order for "Black-Hole" to reach such power it must completely obliterate several dozens or maybe even thousands galaxies, but in the multiverse of probable chances, in my opinion, is highly possible. (http://en.wikipedia.org/wiki/White_hole)

As you aware "Black-Holes" are created by implosion-explosion of super massive stars into "point of convergence" where pressure (acceleration) of Space-Time spherically equal and colossal enough to break Newtonian third low creating conditions where action "in" is no longer balanced by equal and opposite reaction "out". (http://en.wikipedia.org/wiki/Black_hole   https://en.wikipedia.org/wiki/Hawking_radiation)

❖ **Conservation of Energy:**

Is it more economical to melt and reuse steel, aluminum, copper and so on…, or get it from the ground? Of course, we all know, it is a lot more economical to reuse it. Well, it's same with energy. And since everything (including Space-Time) created from energy, it is constantly reused. However, it does not mean energy cannot be created or destroyed. Let say you are in the ocean and using electrolysis to split water. No matter how powerful your apparatus, you will never ever see water disappearing because you are inside and water is everywhere. Furthermore, some of hydrogen and oxygen released will recombine back into water. It is almost the same with energy. Because energy is everywhere and Space-Time itself created from pure energy, it is impossible to destroy it inside our universe (or more accurately multiverse). And as far as creating energy, again, it is a lot easier to reuse and/or release it, but in some cases it actually possible to create energy. Remember, energy is motion-information experienced by us as a force or acceleration (pressure), and by using resonance we can actually create small amounts of energy and use it to reuse/release existing.

Also, I would like to point out that very concentration (accumulation) of motion-information per giving region, however brief, is motion-information on itself (wave_s of wave), another word; a coherence of information is equally an information on itself.

"Nature is pleased with simplicity. And nature is no dummy!" -- **Isaac Newton**

XX.   Quantum Theory:

The very definition of the quantum theory is based on Space-Time being quantize, meaning, you can only jump from point "A" to point "B" without any chance to ever be in between. To me, it's a question of precision. Can we be infinitely precise? And just like with everything the answer would have to be, definite "YES", and most definite "NO". "Yes", because wave is continues' and therefore analog, and "NO", because at some point we would reach limitations of our equipment and human perception, and therefore look for digits or quants. But no matter how weird and confusing the idea of both analog and digital being **one-and-the-same** we, eventually, would have to admit and accept that kind of reasoning. In this chapter, we'll explore some of the "mysteries" of quantum mechanics from revised perception.

1. Probability Clouds: (http://en.wikipedia.org/wiki/Wave%E2%80%93particle_duality)

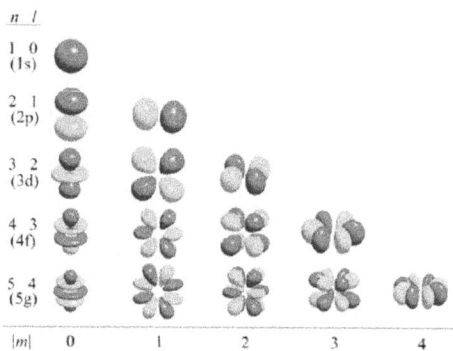

First, let us talk about so called probability cloud. As stated in quantum theory, "electron" in the atom cannot be fully explained as a particle orbiting nucleus and have wave-particle duality property. (http://en.wikipedia.org/wiki/Atomic_orbital) On the picture, you see some examples of "electron" orbitals. I can write several pages explaining in great details why those orbitals looking like balloons and why arrangements of some resembling magnetic field, but it would be a lot more productive if you conduct your own research and draw your own conclusions. All I'm asking is to remember that all "particles" are at constant motion (based on waves actions-reactions), including spin, and spins are creating centrifugal force where it can manifest itself as magnetic fields, and those fields will interact with each other just like permanent magnets. We already discussed how photons (light) and energy trapped around nucleus of the atom can interact and how, regardless of speed, two waves would have measurable interactions only at certain places. (Please refer to chapters "Waves", "Motion-Information", "Magnetism", "Electricity", "Light") As mentioned in chapter "Waves", the wave action cannot be formed without a substance, therefore without trapped energy orbiting (around) nucleus we would never observe those "electron" orbitals. But even with energy, in order to detect "electron" and its behavior we must shine light, where light interacts with energy giving us false perception of particle. (Please refer to chapter "Summary" & Appendix A)

2. Double Slit Experiment: (http://en.wikipedia.org/wiki/Double-slit_experiment)

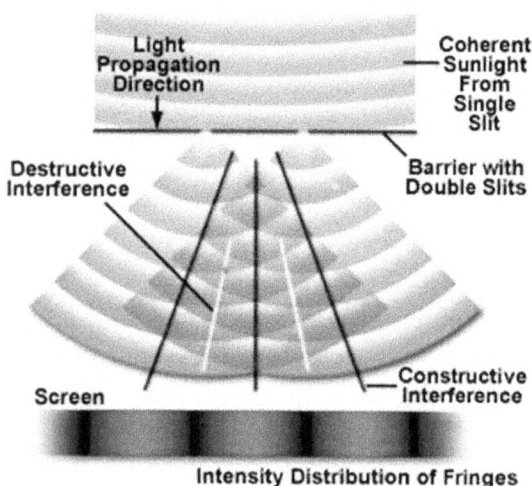

One of so called weird behaviors of the quantum particle that scientists observed is in double slit experiment, where the very act of measuring (observing) changes behavior of particle from analog (continues waves) to digital (particle). But for some reason not many people are paying particular attention to the very act or nature of the observation, rushing to silly conclusions of particles somehow traveling back in Space-Time. This is where we must see the waves not in 2 or even 3 dimensions, but as 4 dimensional spiral (solenoidal) wave. Because as soon as we try to observe behavior of the wave using light, those two spiral crisscrossing with each-other creating appearance of (digital) particle. I would suggest to divide slits plate by a rubber or silicon, cool both plates and measure the changes in temperature of each plate. As so called particles bombard single plate the temperature would slightly increase giving non-evasive tool of spying on them. (Please refer to chapters "Light", "Summary" & Appendix A.5 http://www.youtube.com/watch?v=5ImYXNcQGUc)

3. **Quantum Entanglement:** (http://en.wikipedia.org/wiki/Quantum_entanglement)

The quantum entanglement is one of those so called phenomenon's which would be harder to explain and proof, however, even in this case there are some clues that pointing to the wave behavior. First of all, no one paying particular attention to the entanglements of ONLY oppositely "charged" (span) particles such as "electron" and positron. As I've tried to explain in other chapters, there are no charges but only spins, offsetted from each other by 180° or what would perceived by us left-right (up-down) "directions". Basically, when we talking about entanglements, we are talking about same full wave (particle) as it would be seen from opposite sides. The catch here is in transporting so called entangled particle at speeds far lower than instantaneous, thus negating the idea of instant communication. The true challenge would be in finding ways to influence any "particle" in the universe from your location. Concept known as quantum nonlocality (http://en.wikipedia.org/wiki/Quantum_nonlocality). The quantum nonlocality is another proof of the universe created from one continues wavy substance and good indication of opposite spins ("charges") being actually manifestations of a single full wave observed from two opposite directions. And if you asked, but what about matter-antimatter reaction, it is nothing more than a wave collapse generating rogue wave we perceive as an explosion. To fully comprehend concepts of entanglement and nonlocality, first refer to chapters "Waves", "Motion-Information", "Flip-Flop Continuity" and "Dimensions", and then, think of substance (motion-information without Space-Time), where the only possible "motion" is to change from lowest quantum state to highest and back. The very act of concentration, however brief, leads to instantaneous drop across entire field. Thus by creating entangled pair, we're simply defining where (in Space-Time) concentration and drop would occur. (Please refer to chapter "Summary" & Appendix A.5) (http://en.wikipedia.org/wiki/Rogue_wave http://en.wikipedia.org/wiki/Breaking_wave)

4. **Quantum Bit (qubit):** (http://en.wikipedia.org/wiki/Qubit)

The quantum computing bit or "qubit" is another good example of the universe (multiverse) created from the same wavy substance we call energy, and that energy is motion-information. It is also a good model for observing a full wave and looping circle are being one-and-the-same, and how one always has two states. In our, human, understanding those states would be "HAVES" (logical one or "IS") and "HAVE NOTS" (logical zero or "ISN'T"). In actuality, those states are very rapid changes between high and low saturations. The good example would be flickering of your screen. You don't see it, but every so called static image on your screen actually appearing and disappearing at a very fast rate. Same true in electricity for so called direct current, as in actuality it flows in rapid pulses or waves. It would be hard for you to accept, but even water in your garden hose flows in rapid pulses, as everything is made from spiral circles we perceive as wave-particle. As you know from quantum mechanics, the qubit exists in two states at once (superposition), meaning it is both, logical one and logical zero at once. And you can't even say "at the same time" as it is both space and time at once! The classical explanation of the qubit behavior would be spin-up and spin-down, but as you should know by now, the spins and the waves are actually **ONE-AND-THE-SAME**. (The wave of waves.)

(Please refer to chapters "Waves" and "Summary" & Appendix A.5)

XXI.   Mycelium Field Universe:

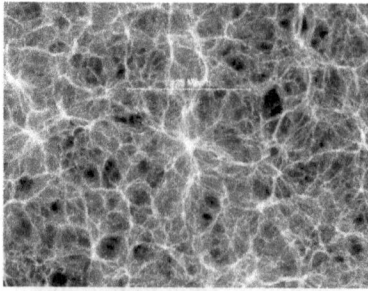

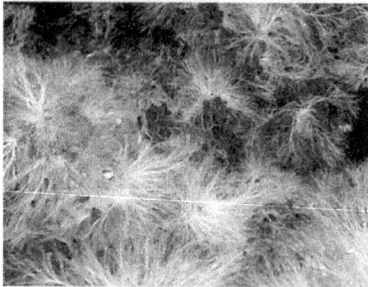

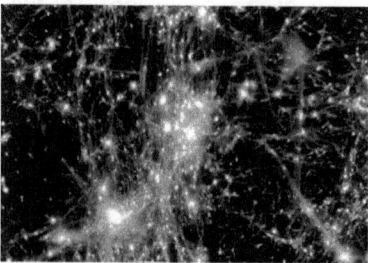

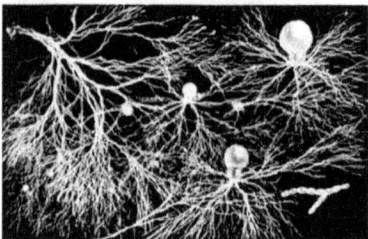

In this chapter, we'll explore our universe and us from a very unappealing perception, comparing the universe and humans (matter) to the mycelium fungus and its fruiting body, the mushroom.

On the pictures you see depictions of our universe based on the galaxies clusters concentrations surrounded by so called "dark matter" and the mycelium fungus, looking somewhat similar.
(http://en.wikipedia.org/wiki/Dark_matter http://en.wikipedia.org/wiki/Gravitational_lens)

Before going any further I'd like to make sure there is no confusion about so called "dark matter". I'm sure at some point in your life you looked at white clouds floating in the blue sky, seen all kinds of shapes, noticing distinct boundaries of the cloud. However, if you fly toward the cloud, trying to reach the boundary, you'll never find where it actually begins, and instead, without even realizing, would fly deep into the cloud itself, only to discover that you are, most likely, already somewhere in the middle of it. All because of false perception, as what, from the distance, looking solid and distinct, in reality could be spread over the great distances being in the state of low saturation. But no matter how low "objects" saturation, it doesn't mean there aren't states of saturation even lower, in some cases, much-much, MUCH lower!

As mentioned many times before, and have been theorized and proven by Albert Einstein, everything is made from the same substance; we call energy, and therefore everything have no choice but to follow same principles taking somewhat familiar geometrical forms. The reason why I choose to compare stars, planets and us humans (matter), to the mushroom is because without observation or study of mycelium there is no obvious connection between fungi, which in most cases looks like white powder web, and its fruiting body the mushroom. However, just like mushrooms all matter has a very real physical connection to the invisible forces we experience every day. This entire work is written with one and only one goal, to prove that there is actual, physical, massive body of all forces, including so called metaphysical as we all just "fruiting bodies" of that (two-dimensional) property we know and experience as **MOTION-INFORMATION**. This connection is not obvious and very counterintuitive, but whether we accept it or not, without proper perception we'll keep wasting energy, waging pitiful wars have been stuck on one planet, where cosmos are filled with riches and the energy is all around us ready and free to use by anyone at any amounts as Space-Time itself is a geometrical structure we recognize as force (shifts of energy), and experience as a multitude of pressures, i.e. **ACCELERATION**.

Pauli Exclusion Principle (http://en.wikipedia.org/wiki/Pauli_exclusion_principle)

Wave diffraction: (http://en.wikipedia.org/wiki/Diffraction   http://www.youtube.com/watch?v=-mNQW5OShMA)

Length Contraction: (http://en.wikipedia.org/wiki/Length_contraction)

Refraction: (http://en.wikipedia.org/wiki/Refraction)

So called "dark matter" surrounding galaxy <u>clusters</u>.

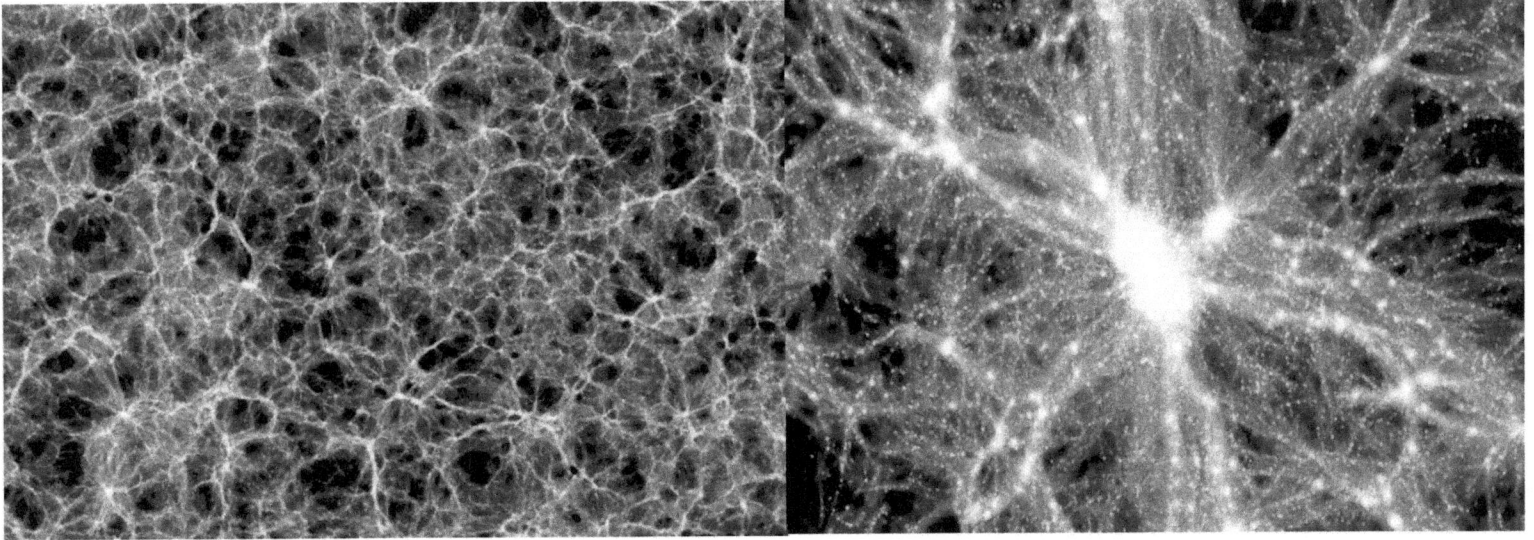

Brain neurons <u>clusters</u>.

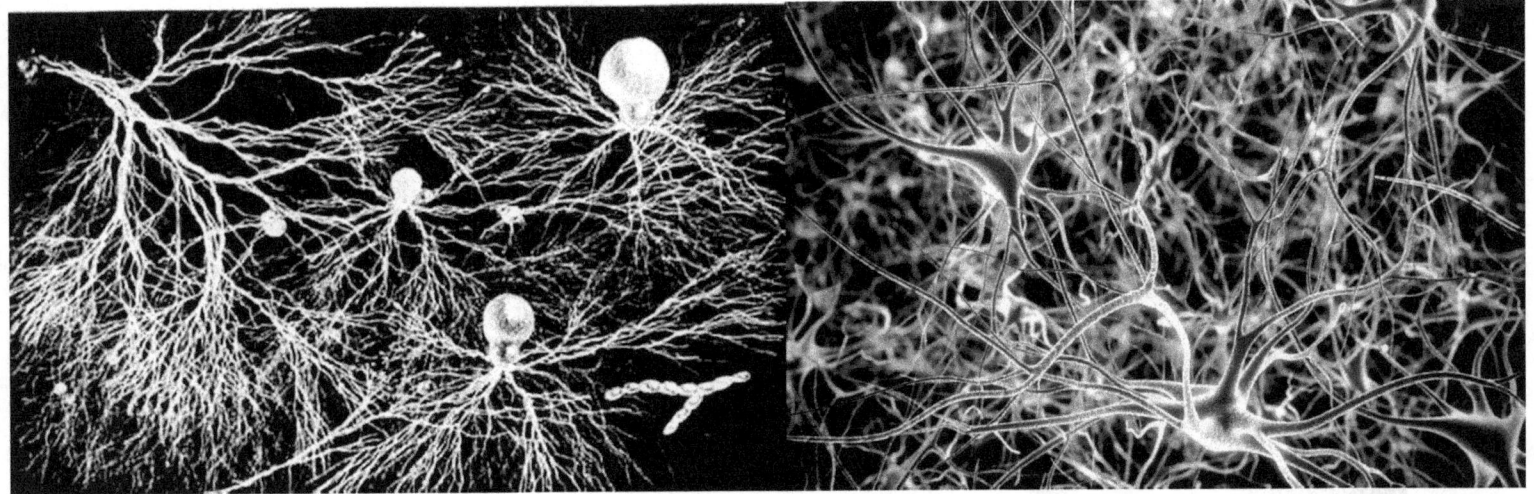

Mycelium fungi <u>clusters</u> and its fruiting body, the mushrooms.

XXII.   Inside the Cocoon:

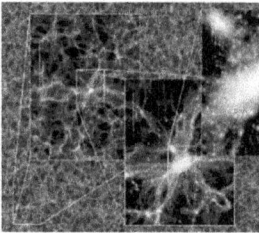

Actually, the more appropriate analogy would be the Russian nesting dolls. If we observe our universe from the concentration (saturation) aspect of the Space-Time (dark matter, gravity, energy) we would notice gradual increase in energy permeation. The least saturated regions would be the Space-Time between galactic clusters, and then between galaxies, the next "step" would be Space-Time around galaxy, then around black hole (depending on distance), and then around stars, and finally for us, humans, it would be the gravity of the planet. But of course it is far from finish as next would be energy between molecules and then around nucleus of the atom and finally neutrons and protons. In terms of Space-Time (energy) density it's exactly like fully assembled Russian dolls. But of course, all we care is gravity, and that is why I called this chapter "Inside the Cocoon".

Why is it so important to see the whole picture and even more important to talk about gravity? That is because natural decay (weak nuclear force, pace of Space-Time) directly tied to the concentration of energy. As you aware, our universe under constant and very rapid inflation (expansion), in fact the speed of expansion is increasing in geometric (spherical) progression, and that means stretching (dropping in saturation) Space-Time. As it occurs the rate of emergence of new energy is no longer sufficient, which means squeezed energy between molecules will accelerate away, leading to natural chemical reactions, and energy around nucleus would also diminish leading to natural decay. As mentioned many times before, everything is interconnected and based on one force, **ACCELERATION**.

Let us try to view our reality (present) not as set of physical objects floating in Space-Time, but as collections of informational values, as our reality nothing more than massive clusters of substance known as motion-information fragmented on so called "standing" waves. Let say there are two virtual routes. If I choose route one, then at some point I will meet that special someone, then at some other point on the road we would either purchase or build our dream house, then have kids, grandkids... But if I choose route two, then I do not meet my significant-other and stay single. Because I'm not a young man, I know with absolute certainty that the person I would've married on route one is already born and have actual physical body as well as my would-be in-laws. As far as the house goes, it could or couldn't exist as I do not know if we would've purchased existing one or build it new. And, of course, to my great sadness, the kids and grandkids have never been materialized.

As you can see from above examples, the "reality" is based on sets of informatively massive values

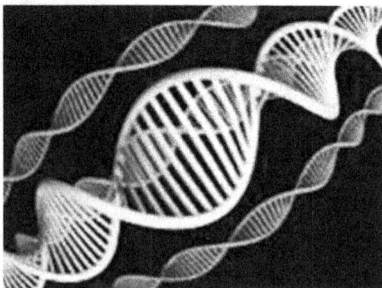

(bodies) coming together, combining (squeezing) within Space-Time, creating, what we call, physical reality. Our DNA is a subset of instructions (information) which are written, just as the rest of our reality, in long **helical** chains. We are not just living inside the "cocoon", but actually, physically connected (plugged-in) to it and interconnected with each other. In other words, we are highly concentrated lumps of the Space-Time (energy), just like tumors. Not because we bad, but because just like cancer and healthy cells are made from the same material (substance).

"If at first the idea is not absurd, then there is no hope for it." -- **Albert Einstein**

XXIII.   Dimensions & Spatial-Geometry:

I left the discussion of dimensions and spatial-geometry (http://en.wikipedia.org/wiki/Shape_of_the_Universe) to the very end of the paper, as this is the most controversial subject because we depend so much not only on the orientations within Space-Time, but rely very heavily on basic locomotion's throughout the spatial-grids. However, just like cyberspace, our, geometrical, universe is also virtual and mathematical. First, let us take a closer look into the binary numeric system and analyze special meaning for numbers 1, 2, 3 and 4. The number "ONE", as you should know by now, is a beginning of everything, as all-that-we-are is created from the same singular substance, which is indissoluble and whole. If it is indivisible then why there are so many formulas in physics and mathematics where "ONE" is divided by something? And that is why and where number "TWO" is getting its special meaning, because the only way "ONE" can gain any meaningful informational (mathematical) "worth" is by "EXISTING" or "HAVE" (logical 1) and "NOT EXISTING" or "HAVE NOT" (logical 0). But remember, "HAVE NOT" doesn't mean absolute vacuum as vacuum itself is something. Instead picture logical zero as lower saturation of the same substance, similar to digital electronics where a single memory cell is occupied by same substance

4	2	1	
0	0	0	0
0	0	1	1
0	1	0	2
0	1	1	3
1	0	0	4
1	0	1	5
1	1	0	6
1	1	1	7

but at different voltage (pressure). Combined, those two statements will give us number "THREE" where "ONE" would be perceived as average, neutral or "ORIGIN" (medium) energy (value) and "TWO" as "Potentials" or possible extremes (high-low), making number "THREE" into a representation of the superposition fluctuation. The number "THREE" has special meaning because it represents an actual and for the first-time physical **two-dimensional** frequencies ("particles") which have ability to move with the speed of light, making them outside of any four-dimensional Space-Time constraints, where the only way for them to slowdown (red-shifted) is by interaction (proximity) with other waves ("particles"). If you analyze the standard model theory of quantum mechanics, you'll notice **THREE** energy regimes (low, medium and high) for each of the **FOUR** fundamental particles (up quark, down quark, electron and neutrino), for a total of TWELVE, plus symmetric counterparts making it into **TWENTY FOUR**. As you can see in the table there are TWENTY FOUR cells of ones and zeroes, where they are arranged into harmonically (right to left) structured waves (top to bottom) of increasing wavelength and decreasing frequencies. The next observation is very controversial, but could bear some truth to it. As you know there are THREE higher frequencies beyond visual range (ultra violet, x-ray, and gamma rays), THREE types of radiation (Alpha, Beta, Gamma), THREE basic colors (red, green, blue (R.G.B.)), THREE "flavors" of neutrinos (electron, muon and tau), THREE quarks for each of subatomic "particles". At this point I would theorize that quarks, neutrinos and WIMPs are forms of gamma rays created due to collapse (implosion) of the wave and all other radiations, including the entire spectrum of colors, are "red-shifted" aftereffects due to (and governed by) the density of a given medium, where (depending on saturation) aging-time is slowed down and spatial-geometry length is contracted, in agreement with General Relativity Theory lensing effect. If the above statement is too controversial for you, consider this; there is a crustacean known as snapping or pistol shrimp which shoots jet of water by snapping its claw. The jet is so powerful it creates cavity bubble, where the entire mass of water, due to pressure, forcing the bubble to collapse, producing bright light, extremely high temperatures and deafening sound which shrimp uses to stun or kill its pray (http://en.wikipedia.org/wiki/Fundamental_frequency).

But enough sad about number THREE and it is time to talk in great details about the special meaning of number **FOUR** as our entire reality practically permeates by that number including us.

To better understand this entire chapter it would be advisable to learn as much as possible about fractals and fractal geometry as well as study next chapter "Summary".

(http://en.wikipedia.org/wiki/Fractal   http://en.wikipedia.org/wiki/Mandelbrot_set   http://www.youtube.com/watch?v=LemPnZn54Kw http://www.youtube.com/watch?v=5qXSeNKXNPQ) Just for the sake of argument, let's forget everything we learned so far about the constant conically spiral motions and talk about the circle. You see, the full 360° circle, logically (philosophically), doesn't make sense. We are starting the journey at 0° and on completion, or closing of the circle at 360°, we are actually ending at the same 0° point. Basically, there is no logical reason to execute a full turn if we'll end-up right where we already were. Whenever there is a military command "about face", the soldier makes 180° turn, which in four-dimensional geometry would be only half circle or radiant π (Pi). If you need more evidence in physics and math formulas I suggest watching this YouTube channel http://www.youtube.com/user/DrPhysicsA?feature=watch. Pay attention to lessons about waves and especially "standing" waves (http://en.wikipedia.org/wiki/Standing_wave http://www.youtube.com/watch?v=jSLw01C9Pv8 http://en.wikipedia.org/wiki/Wavenumber https://en.wikipedia.org/wiki/Angular_frequency). The point I'm trying to make, is that the two-dimensional (original) circle actually is a 180° and representation of, what's known in quantum physics, superposition principle (http://en.wikipedia.org/wiki/Superposition_principle), where 0° and 90° are indications of flip point. Look at the pictures and accept the "X" axis or 0° as so called quantum field (http://en.wikipedia.org/wiki/Quantum_field_theory) in lowest quantum state or logical zero, and 90° as highest quantum state or logical one (https://en.wikipedia.org/wiki/Quantum_state). An empty memory cell, philosophically,

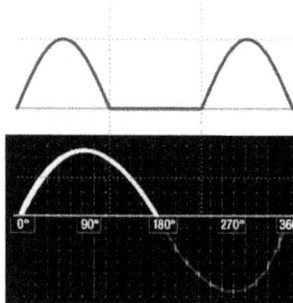

is in a superposition state, as it can hold either logical one or logical zero. We would call that, "state indeterminate", simply because we accept the idea of nothing, where in reality, there is no such thing and there is always something. We perceive vacuum as lack of air (gases) knowing very well that everything is made of the same energy and lack of matter does not constitute lack of energy. Therefore, geometry, dimensions or Space-Time is not a measurement of distances, curvatures, flows or accumulations, but measurements of efficiencies. There can NEVER be 3, 9, 10 or 11 dimensions, as dimension, like binary system, would always double. (Please do not mistake availability of dimensions and usage of them.) Each shifted position (status) would always have two states of existence. The only reason 360° circle makes any sense, is because we are constantly moving (forward) in the four-dimensional substance of Space-Time (converting two-dimensional motion-information (energy) into four-dimensional "digitized" substance (force) i.e. acceleration), meaning we are NEVER at the same point in cosmic Space-Time. As you aware, there are three-axial spatial-geometry plus aging-time. But why FOUR? Why this number keeps repeating itself in many different disciplines including power? Why majority of animals (mammals, birds, reptiles) have FOUR limbs? Why rectangle and square shapes are most used? Why there are FOUR fundamental forces, FOUR states of matter (solid, liquid, gas, and plasma), FOUR fundamental particles, FOUR DNA organic bases (G A C T)? Is it coincidence that subatomic particles do FOUR motions at once (curl, vibrate, wobble, and move away from the center of the "Big-Bang" Inflation)... It all has to do with efficiency and we need a minimum of four to function. As mentioned, dimensions are not a measurement of Space-Time, but descriptions of efficiency. For example, if you are trying to meet someone, but know only street name, let's call it "X", your chances to meet is less than ≈ 0.0000001%. But if you know intersecting street "Y", your chances will increase to over twenty percent. By adding time for the meeting, your chances increase to well over eighty percent and so on... Now, let us evaluate another example. How long and how well can you stand on one foot? Not as well and as long as on two because by removing one leg, instead of FOUR points of support, you'll have only three. Yes, I said **FOUR**! And what are those other two points beside your legs? Obviously, if we didn't have gravity, we would not be able to walk as we do. Thus, we have three, two legs and gravity, where is number four? Well, if you know anatomy, there is such thing as vestibular apparatus. If I get two wheeled bike it would keep falling because it has only three points of support (two wheels and gravity) and unless we provide one more, either a natural vestibular system or gyroscope or angular velocity/angular momentum (http://en.wikipedia.org/wiki/Angular_velocity), it will not stand on two wheels. But is it easier to keep balance sitting on the bike without or with some motion? Of course, while moving (balancing). And now, we have two wheels, gravity, vestibular system and motion. If you counted it makes five points and if we add angular velocity we'll get six. The more points, or dimensions, more efficient the ride. Same can be done with power. To properly calculate consumption of power we must take into consideration pressure (volt), volume (current), resistance (friction) and aging-time. By adding fifth dimension, for example resonance, we can come up with more efficient systems for power generation/consumption and management. At the beginning of this chapter I advised you to learn about fractal (harmonic) geometry, also in chapter "Motion-Information" I (humorously) mentioned race of intelligent snails and as a part of the title included phrase: "Escargot law of extremely slow motions". Actually, there are deeper reasons why I choose snails as a sort of representatives. If you look at the pictures of snail shells you'll see good examples of fractal geometry and natures' tendency to curl. In fact, fractal geometry is based on curls as it is constructed by loops. Now, let us talk about extremely slow motions. As you know, it takes 365.25 days for the Earth to go around the Sun and there are 360° in full (four-dimensional) circle. If you search for references you'll find extensive and very convincing explanations why there is absolutely no correlation between those values. However, it wasn't always the case. At some overly distant past, our galaxy and therefore our solar system (including Sun) were more compact (following Einsteins' time dilation and length contraction) and it took Earth 360 days to travel around the Sun. That compactness would also cause higher gravitational strength and would create larger animals (like dinosaurs) as they would need bigger muscles and denser bone structures. (http://en.wikipedia.org/wiki/Gigantism) Makes you think about Plato's "Atlantis" (http://en.wikipedia.org/wiki/Atlantis), lost civilizations of Eurasia, Africa, America and other early continents like Pangaea... (https://en.wikipedia.org/wiki/Pangaea) In chapter "Inside the Cocoon" we explored different saturations (densities) of spatial-regions as well as replenishments of spatial-concentrations thru natural chemical reactions, natural decay, atomic fissions and fusions. All those processes do slow down expansion of Space-Time to the almost "standing" crawl, nevertheless Space-Time inside galaxies does expanding and as you "wasted" your "time" reading this chapter, your body and everything around you did inflate as well as speeded-up in aging-time by exceedingly miniscule amounts. Early people in "Old Testament" are described to live for hundreds of years, decreasing in longevity with each generation. I'm far from theology, UFO researchers and other occults, however, logically, there is a great possibility that Earth journeyed much-much faster around the Sun and human years were counted by the number of harvests, which in some parts of the world could be 2 or even 3 per Earth revolution around the Sun. I hope you realize that it is 0° and 90°, or the flips, that made geometrical (spatial) points possible as without those there will be no separation on regions and therefore no Space-Time, where a multitude of points are responsible for increased or diminished efficiencies. Same reason why AC current and higher frequencies are more efficient in transmitting electrical charges over the great distances than DC electricity.

❖ The power of stop: Remember; *it's not the fall that kills, but the abrupt __STOP!__*

As you know from history, when people try to invent motion pictures, at first, they would continuously spin the film, and as a result picture came out all smudged and blurry. Only after several attempts people understood that sharp and clear moving picture is a series of still photographs. Moreover, in order to view the movie as clear as on the film, it must be shown as certain amounts of **stops** and go motions (per second). Throughout this theory you've been reading that everything is in constant (continues) motion because energy itself is motion-information experienced by us as force, and it is customary (mathematically) to think that power is a force (pressure) multiplied by mass. However, without **stops** (flip) **points** energy would've never transformed into force and universe (multiverse) would remain just featureless continuity as, strictly speaking, **stops** are the original and true vacuum (The Zero-Point Energy Concept: http://en.wikipedia.org/wiki/Zero-point_energy). As you've been reading, gravity is a flow (pressure) of the Space-Time ("Big-Bang" inflation shock wave). If we learn to stop that flow, we'll achieve true antigravity technology. The more stop points per unit of measure, the more efficient and powerful the appliance.

XXIV.   Human Psyche & Philosophy:

Let us discuss human psyche, especially about individuality and why it is so important to us (humans), and our natural tendency to particulate our world. The concept of being an individual and a concept of the ownership are two most primal instincts we people have. Those values are burned into our psyche and in most societies are considered to be most fundamental and highly guarded values. We, people, like (and in some cases need) the idea of being independent, unattached entities that would possess individual items, properties, life stocks... Those egoistic values define us as species of individual entities, give us a false sense of being in control of the situation, in control of the possessions, in control of the life itself. While those prime instincts are helping us to cope with the reality, giving us a sense of security and predictability, being the only species on Earth with the ability to rationalize and discard false perceptions, we must accept the real possibility, that everything in this reality is interconnected and that is philosophy, thoughts, perceptions, force and energy have physical or more accurately two-dimensional metaphysical bodies that are just as real as matter in all its forms and shapes.

❖ **Philosophy:**

As you aware, every law, all rules and regulations are created by humans, for one and ONLY one purpose and that is to box you within some confinements, to create walls for your mind and physical body.

While I would never argue on the importance of having the laws, rules and regulations, as we, people, not only need those limitations for the societies to function properly, but we even crave them, as most people are followers by nature, and it is easier (less stressful) to live life within rules as those give sense (false or otherwise) of security, and for some, even purpose. Said all that, I must point out, that nature does not have laws, rules and regulations. Animals, especially birds, crossing borders, fly from country to country, from one continent to another, without passports, visas, permissions or "red tapes". Sure, there are some guidelines (instincts), flock and pack dynamics, as all social animals also can be divided on leaders and followers, however, none of those are "set in stone", written as final and unbreakable. In human history there were laws and enforcements which by today's standards would be considered criminal, like, for example, protection of the ownership of slaves, or discrimination of minorities and women... Whenever archeologists want to learn about ancient times they start digging down, and the first things they usually discover are the roofs of archaic civilizations. At one time in our distant history, ancient people would have to look up, clime ladders or ropes, build scaffoldings in order to reach those heights, but today, we are using that knowledge as foundations of our societies. It is same in physics; we are building an understanding of our reality, stocking new perceptions, and new concepts on top of the old. Each discovery and each new theory are just another stepping stone in our struggle to understand nature.

<u>Therefore, what we call "Laws of Physics" in actuality are just "Foundations of Perceptions", fluid and dynamic (same as Space-Time), guidelines to achieve new understanding, and, as a result, technologies.</u>

❖ **Universal Subconscious:**

Many people asking if there some kind of universal intelligence. Not the creationists, but the emergent (developed) one, due to longevity and complexity of the universe. My short answer would have to be **I don't know**. However, let me describe the scenario which might shed some light on the subject. Obviously we, people, consider ourselves intelligent beings and, as such, can influence our own bodies thru exercises, food, medications and other chemical and mineral compounds, chosen lifestyles, meditations and more... But have you ever cared for each individual cell in your body? Have you ever tried to influence singular, particular cell? Obviously the answer would be "NO". We simply do not recognize each individual cell as of any special importance. We care about groups of cells like, for example; major organs, muscle groups, bone structure and density... In the meantime, each individual cell is evolving (growing), reproducing (dividing and in some cases mutating) and dying, just like we do. Inside your house up to 90% of dust are human dead skin cells. Therefore, in my opinion, purely following cold hard logic, if there is such emerged subconscious intelligence, each of us simply isn't important enough to even bother to influence individually. Unfortunately majority of people are narrow minded and simply cannot cope with notion of triviality.

Remember opening phrase from the "Abstract" chapter?

"Perhaps, the greatest challenge for us, humans, is humility."

"Truth is ever to be found in the simplicity, and not in the multiplicity and confusion of things."
-- Isaac Newton

XXV.   Summary:

Let us summarize transitioning process from one-dimensional (incoherent) substance, we perceive as informational constituent, into two-dimensional (poly-coherent) energy, called in this theory motion-information, **shifting** into four-dimensional (cubically or symmetrically opposing-coherent) force, known as waves, Space-Time, dark energy, dark matter, gravity, pressure, mass, aether, i.e. - **ACCELERATION**, and finally into multi-dimensionally coherent (harmonic) mass (saturation) and matter we calling our reality. The graphs you'll see in this chapter are **NOT** to be taken "literally" and meant to be just an interface helping explain (translate) conversion processes. (http://en.wikipedia.org/wiki/Quantum_decoherence) As mentioned in chapter "Introduction", there are no such things as charged particles or quarks, then, what actually exists? Well, in actuality the only metaphysical substance that is real is ENERGY, which we also recognize as **INFORMATION**. However, this one-dimensional substance by itself is a meaningless, and only becomes (could be considered as) two-dimensional energy by constant fluctuation (increase) in density, also known as coherence of information. (http://en.wikipedia.org/wiki/Coherent_information) That is why in this theory I call it MOTION-INFORMATION. As we constantly moving in aging-time <u>seemingly</u> without moving in spatial-geometry, so is the information can change (increase) its coherence only thru motion, without actual repositioning within Space-Time (especially when such substance doesn't yet exists). Actually, in our four-dimensional universe, as we moving forward in aging-time we are also in constant motion forward in spatial-geometry, where continuous expansion of the universe and therefore repositioning of each and all objects (including us) within Space-Time is **new information**, and that is how every rock, every grain of dust and even so called empty Space-Time itself **creates** new energy. The unusual property of mentioned one-dimensional substance, from our point of view, would be the immediate drop or so called quantum decoherence across entire field which is permeating throughout countless universes. After all, if I procure a bucket of water from the ocean, we would never register any drop of water level across Entire Ocean. Such concept of instantaneous, faster than speed of light, drop across entire (from our point of view, infinite) substance is very alien to us as we live in the world bound by magnetic fields (viscosity), hold and kept in concentrations by various pressures (acceleration) and driven (whether we wanted or not) by constant and only forward motion in Space-Time. (Remember, just as we need atmospheric pressure to keep liquids in our bodies from boiling, all atoms and atomic structures need Space-Time (gravity, dark matter, dark energy, i.e. acceleration) to exert pressure and slow-down (in some cases stop completely) decaying process known as weak nuclear force.) Such confusion can be easily overcome by conducting very simple experiment. Make a sloping surface with vertical stopper on the lower end of the surface, and place several balls in the row on the surface, as you can see on the below picture. If you remove first (lowest) ball next to the vertical stopper, all balls will move simultaneously. All at once, even if the surface and the row of "balls" are several billion-trillion

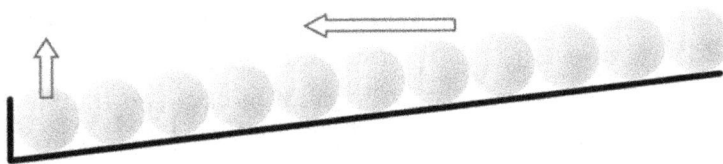

miles long. Obviously we are talking about one-dimensional substance perceived by us as information. This substance, in actuality, has absolutely no informative (data) meaning (at least to us) as it is completely uniformed and has no distinctive futures until it fluctuates, increasing its coherence, cozying simultaneous drop across entire substance. I intentionally not using words like "point" or "section", as this substance is everywhere and nowhere-in-particular. However alien to us that kind of perception, fluctuations of coherence is possible without distinct locale. This <u>fluctuated</u> substance would be our two-dimensional motion-information. It is just two-dimensional precisely because there are only increased and neutral coherent states. The decreased state (also known as negative energy) is not yet possible because drop occurs simultaneously across entire substance making the rest of the substance into neutral or average, uniformed state of coherence. You would probably recognize this fluctuating substance as fluctuating membrane or "Brane" in the M-theory (http://en.wikipedia.org/wiki/Introduction_to_M-theory   http://en.wikipedia.org/wiki/M-theory) proposed by Edward Witten (http://en.wikipedia.org/wiki/Edward_Witten). The next logical event would be the vShift into four-dimensional substance we recognize as Space-Time, mass, waves, force, pressure..., i.e. - **ACCELERATION**. However, this shift requires emergence of symmetrically (to the increased) diffusion (or decoherence), making it into four distinct states, <u>**highest**</u> - (positive pick), <u>**lowest**</u> - (negative pick), **neutral** - (average, balanced or concept of zero in math) and <u>**transitional**</u> (aging-time). This shift into four-dimensional (digitized) substance would be possible only if two increased states occuring at close enough proximity from each other, where such vicinity would force constituent, between, to drop below the lowest state of the entire bulk of a given substance. On the below graph you can see the approximate representation of those transformations. The punctured line is representing the original one-dimensional state where only

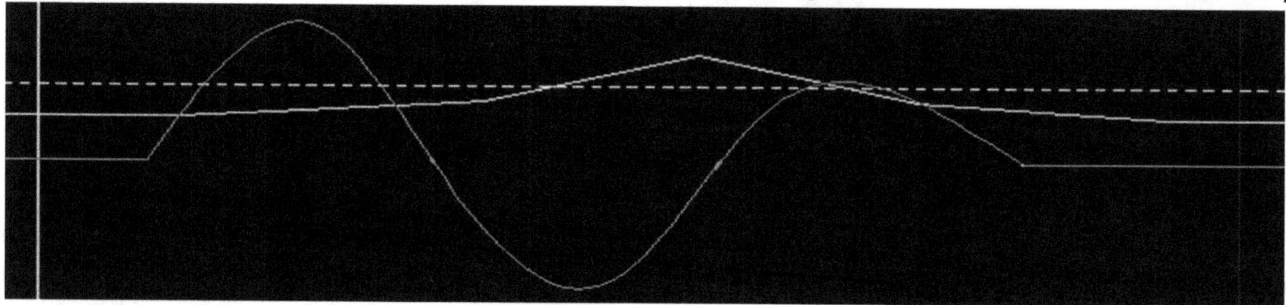

one geometrical possibility of 0° state is feasible. The next line looking like a mountain would be the two-dimensional status, triggering immediate drop across entire field, with two geometrical possibilities, 0° to positive 90° and back, making it into 180° circled geometry, without any transitioning (aging) possibilities because any increase (level) in density regardless of the volume is instantaneous and inert. And finally, the full wave with positive to negative regions would be our four-dimensional force where we have four geometrical possibilities, 0° to positive 90° and back, plus 0° to negative 90° and back, creating full 360° spherical geometry and <u>spirally</u> arranged (http://en.wikipedia.org/wiki/Phyllotaxis) structures (the waves interference pattern). As mentioned before, if you analyze any power to its very core, you'll discover that it works on one very simple principle, where higher pressure (density, saturation, coherence) region forcing itself into lower pressure region in order to equalize both. This seemingly simple, yet extremely important, principle accepted in modern physics as the Entropic Force (http://en.wikipedia.org/wiki/Entropic_force) and also considered as Thermodynamical <u>Equilibrium</u> (http://en.wikipedia.org/wiki/Thermodynamic_equilibrium), where we would recognize geometrically (spherically) shaped wavy (spiral) structures. It is spherical in geometry because the outer "membrane" of the structures in all directions is the highest saturation (density) region (or positive energy) and the inner cavity is the lowest saturation (diffusion or so called negative energy) region (or the negative energy). But more importantly, because it is structured (digitized) substance, it gives the possibility where we can recognize two "entities" absolutely vital to our perception of Space-Time. The first one would be points in spatial-geometry (or grid structures or stops, also can be viewed as zero point energy), and the second would be the force, we perceive as pressure or more accurately **ACCELERATION**.

This, geometrical, arrangement creates perfect condition for the very sudden and powerful implosions as observed in (liquids, gases and plasma) cavitation bubbles, where, in some cases, it could lead to the explosions or inflations as with so called "Big-Bang". It is not immediately obvious, but all explosions occurring only after very sudden and powerful implosions and it all has to do with action-reaction pair. Remember, for every action "IN" there is an equal and opposite reaction "OUT", where two cancelling each-other, until something gives-up (implodes) where action "IN" suddenly collapses, thus giving chance to reaction "OUT" temporary but powerful (massive per tiny period of Space-Time) advantage. You can have implosions without explosion but **NEVER** the other way around, and yes, only implosions are producing bright "bluish" light (gamma radiation). How all those actions leading into emergence of matter? (http://en.wikipedia.org/wiki/Blue_giant) For that to occur, nature would needed truly enormously powerful event such as "Big-Bang" where some of the imploded (collapsed on itself) bubbles (waves), at and close, to the center of so called "White-Hole" would not be able to radiate out, due to enormous overall mass (external pressure) of the entity. Basically, all those gamma radiations close to the center would be contained or lens (lensing effect http://en.wikipedia.org/wiki/Gravitational_lens) into balanced (compressed) state of the full wave, converting it into massive (so called positively "charged") entities we recognize as protons (http://en.wikipedia.org/wiki/Proton). (Please remember, each single full wave has geometrical shape of the sphere, but constructed (propagates) as conically shaped logarithmic spiral, because, within four-dimensional substance, it's always wants to inflate.) Of course, the only way such enormously tight squeezing could be achieved if that energy "string" (the full wave) would curl on itself, as curling is form of single full wave which is bends onto itself, loosing concepts of Space-Time within its internal structure. (Please refer to chapter "Flip-Flop Continuity") As you know all super massive "Black-Holes" radiate extremely powerful gamma rays, because they are, while enormously compressed, not massive enough to contain gamma radiation produced by surrounding magnetic field. I should point out that "Black-Holes" in actuality neither "black" nor "hole". The reason we call it "black" because all we can detect is glowing halo of destroyed and super-heated matter (converted, as it falls, into pure plasma) which is surrounding (orbiting) the compression far before it reaches the event-horizon (point of no return), after which it streams like a single indistinguishable "blob" of super-duper heated "liquid" plasma (no viscosity) where Space-Time is no longer has any meaning as it being replaced (converted) by "liquid" two-dimensional substance. This is where any data saved on the surface (above event-horizon) is being destroyed. Unfortunately, for us, that data, which is partial but only useful information, is no longer reconstitutable into physical entity even if we theoretically switch Space-Time into "reverse gear", precisely because mentioned two-dimensional "blob" has no such concept. Falling into "Black-Hole" is truly and most definitely only one-way trip and that is why it is a "hole". As you know, all "Black-Holes" are created by implosion-explosion of super massive stars (http://en.wikipedia.org/wiki/Neutron_star) where Space-Time is squeezed into super-duper heated and "liquid" "point of no return" so small and so dense, that the flow of Space-Time is simply stops, because it is pushing (accelerating) onto itself equally and spherically, which means one way "door", where everything checks in and nothing comes out. ("Welcome to the Hotel California" https://www.youtube.com/watch?v=h0G1Ucw5HDg) Even smaller rogue "Black-Holes" which don't have matter to gobble-up will trap all (including all "electromagnetic" radiations such as light) and would be detectable only by so called gravitational lensing effect. But enough about "Black-Holes" and ultimate destruction. Now that we know how protons where created, let see how it acquires "cloud" of energy around itself and why mass (which is quantity) and acceleration or pressure (which is force) are actually **one-and-the-same**. Due to proton's constant curling onto itself, it creates barrier where inflating spherical acceleration cannot flow thru, and since that pressure is constant and balanced each proton somewhat acts as tiny femtoscopical "Black-Holes" (http://en.wikipedia.org/wiki/Femto- http://en.wikipedia.org/wiki/Micro_black_hole). But remember, this curling or spin occurs not in two but in all **FOUR** axis, meaning direction of the spin is in constant change (flips) similar to what labeled as "Dzhanibekov Effect" or "Tennis Racket Theorem".

(http://en.wikipedia.org/wiki/Tennis_racket_theorem   http://en.wikipedia.org/wiki/Vladimir_Dzhanibekov https://www.youtube.com/watch?v=dL6Pt1O_gSE   https://www.youtube.com/watch?v=UPzbuUMPLJ4)

You should also remember; that spin, and therefore flips, occurring at extremely fast paces where distances are almost non-existent, which leads to extremely fast motion, making proton into "solid" spherical ball we all recognize as particle. Spinning, floating, wobbling and changing location within Space-Time. Being focal and spherical point of convergence, protons are "forcing" surrounding pressure of Space-Time to pile-up around itself into halo or cloud of compressed flux which "vortexes" (due to dragging effect) creating funnel effect (due to centrifugal acceleration), we recognize as magnetic field, where flow of flux from pole to pole creates additional interferences leading to higher density. (Please refer to chapters "Mass & Matter", "Gravity", "Magnetism", "Space-Time" & "The Substance") The "solid" objects, while being very real to us, from the natures' point of view are just illusions created by harmonically arranged ultra-high frequencies created by extreme pressures and vibrations (heat). If you have repeatedly jumping tennis ball at low pace and you want to move your hand crossing path of the ball without interference, it would be fairly easy to "time-it", but if balls frequency would increase to several hundred or hundred-billions per second, the entire path would look to us like solid "wall" where "particle" seemingly occurring in every point throughout the pass at once. Similarly, our entire Universe (Multiverse) is created from one single "entity", jumping (quantum tunneling) creating appearance of lumpy Space-Time. Whenever you are observing on computer screen or TV monitor video or even "static" image, you are (seemingly) looking at whole picture. But it is NOT how it constructed. That entire image delivered to the screen (left to right) pixel by pixel and (top to bottom) line by line and static frame by static frame. If you have ever experienced flickering of the screen, that is because of the relatively slow refresh rate.

Please remember, this entire book and all included materials were put together not to give you ready and absolute answers, but to let you look at our universe from an alternative perception, and to provide the starting "points" where you should conduct your own research and arrive to your own conclusions.

Self-education not only the best way to learn, but it also gives an individual sense of pride and self-respect.

XXVI.   Conclusion:

In conclusion I would like to emphasize that everything you see around, and your body, is a collection of waves, compressed and spliced, on harmonic frequencies, "suspended" ("frozen"), from our point of view, in Space-Time, and because everything is created from same substance we call energy (motion-information), our entire universe, from everything small to everything big, is governs by same processes, and by observing nature, and adjusting perceptions, we could and should understand fundamental works of all. I'd like to point out that our universe is both a lot simpler and a lot more complex than we've ever perceive, and Newtonian laws of motion equally true for everything big and everything small, precisely because they are motion-information. The uncertainty principle, known in Newtonian Physics as "potential", is both applicable and not, just the same for classical and quantum mechanics. As mentioned many times before, contradiction (which is other word for complexity) and simplicity are the Yin-Yang (Flip-Flop) in scientific and philosophical understanding of the universe. If you paid attention, the entire discussion was about various multitudes of frequencies and how we, humans, perceive those occurrences (http://en.wikipedia.org/wiki/Holographic_principle).

As our universe (multiverse) moves forward (repositioning) within Space-Time, it constantly creates new motion-information which is perceived by us as energy, where that energy is geometrically shaped into force, and force in mass gives us power. We can easily accept the idea that new information can be created, but can NEVER be destroyed, because it is part of our everyday reality.

These days, both, engineers and scientist officially admitted that with all our modern technology it would be impossible to build great pyramids of Egypt, however, our ancestors did not have LAWS of physics and therefore did not know what is possible and impossible.

It all comes down to our perception, of reality, of understanding, of possibilities. Our both strange and ordered (mathematical) universe should be perceived not only from cold mathematical calculations, but also from philosophical and maybe even spiritual view **(please do not mistake spirituality with believes and especially religion)**. I'm not claiming to be completely accurate on every single topic, (after all I'm also only human with my, human, four-dimensional perceptions) but as I was writing this theory, it got increasingly obvious that it is not about being "true" or "false", as we are actually always right and wrong at once, but is about finding appropriate words to describe events and processes, words, that are already familiar to others, as many of us got use to think in stereotypes and have very hard time to restructure the way we comprehend the reality. The theory itself was written not to give absolute, definite answers on all questions, but to give a chance to look at our universe from different perspective, to ask questions that are, maybe, outside of your comfort zone.

While writing this theory I also work on developing practical technology which would make possible to convert gravity (Space-Time i.e. **ACCELERATION**) directly into **unlimited** amounts of electrical charges at any location including "micro gravity". I am, by far, not the first (nor-last) person to discover those possibilities. For now, let us say – it's time for humanity to join cosmic communities of the "Type One" civilizations, where energy available to anyone[1], anywhere[2], anytime[3] and at any amounts[4], and where such technologies like antigravity, warp propulsion, asteroid mining, terraforming and colonization of planets are everyday reality.

Appendix A: Practical Applications:

1. Electrical Transformer-Generator: (http://en.wikipedia.org/wiki/Transformer)

Whether you believe it or not, all electrical transformers work not by transforming power from one coil to another, but by actually **GENERATING** electricity, **exactly** like mechanical generators. Before detailed explanation on the actual work of transformers, I'd like to point out that you don't necessarily have to have two coils. On the diagrams below you can see examples of what known as autotransformers where

Autotransformer

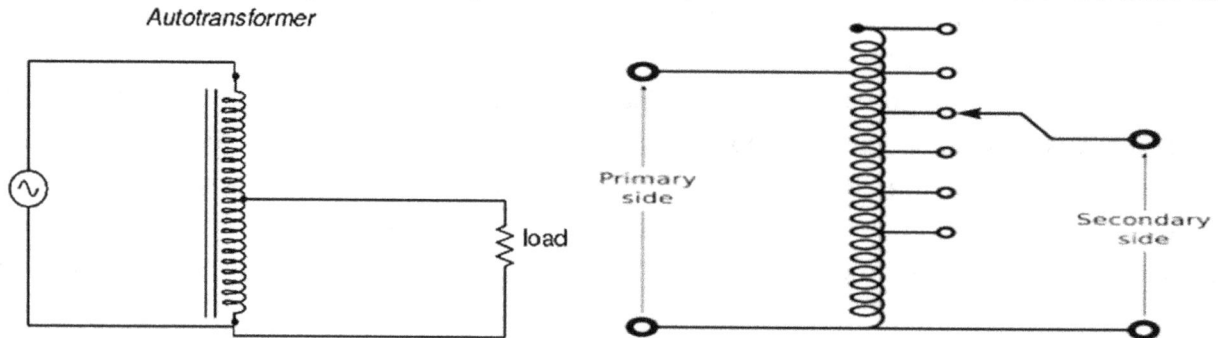

single coil is both, primary and secondary segment. The drawback of autotransformers is inability of noise cancelation unlike two coiled design. Why is it so important for us to understand this concept, and how is it transformer **GENERATES** electricity? On the other diagrams below you see design of basic AC (Alternating Current) electricity generator, where coil of wire is spinning inside magnetic field created by two permanent magnets. You can also see corresponding sine wave generated inside the coil.

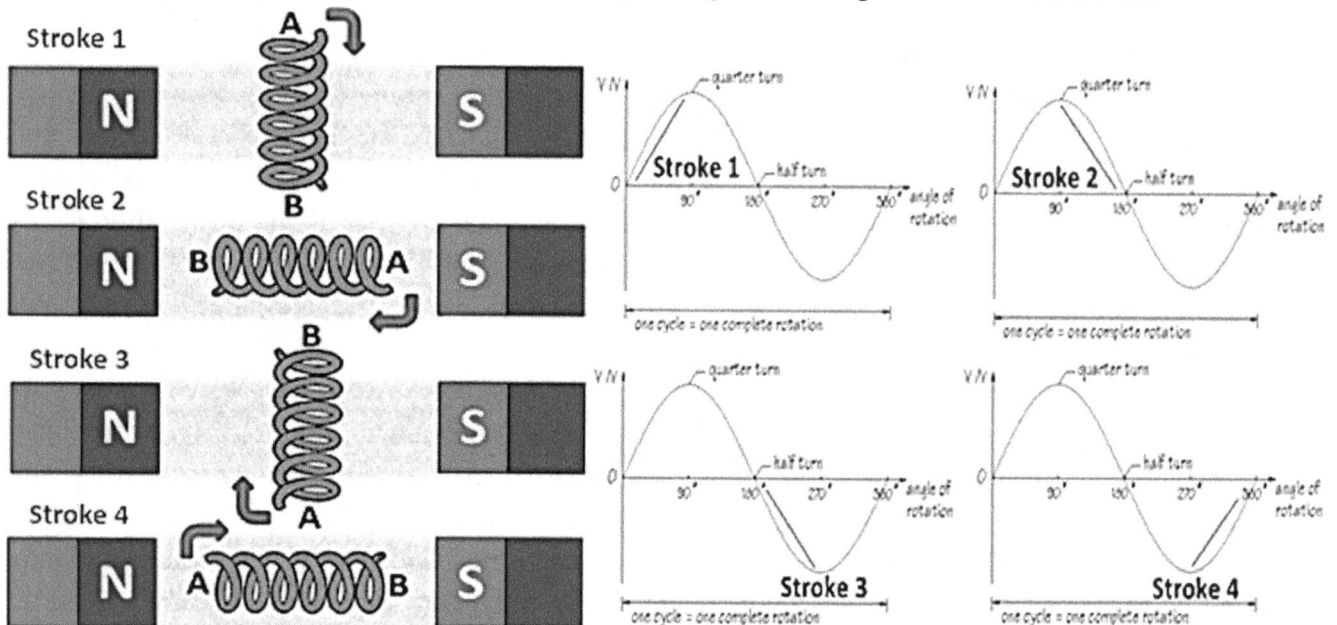

I broke circular motion of the coil on four strokes (quarter turns) so it would be easier to understand how mechanical (rotating) motion of the coil being repeated (mirrored) inside electricity generating wire. *(Please refer to section "Preface" and chapters "Waves", "Motion-Information", "The Energy", "The Force", "Gravity", "Magnetism", "Electricity", "Light", "Space-Time" and "The Bridge")*

Basically, you can consider the magnetic field between magnets as underwater current (pressure) where spinning (rotating) coil is simply changing the interaction rate (strength) applied by that current.

But can we replace permanent magnets with electromagnets? Sure we can. There is no difference whether magnetic field created by permanent or electro magnets. By the way, that is how the alternator in your car is made. There are two coils, one works as electromagnet when DC (direct current) electricity is applied to it, and second is a generating coil. Now, if all we need is to change the interaction strength then why not instead of DC apply AC to the electromagnet(s) and generate electricity without mechanical motion? This concept of generating electricity without mechanical motion and using only one coil (like in autotransformers) was first pioneered and somewhat understood by **Nicola Tesla** in his famous tesla **coil** (http://en.wikipedia.org/wiki/Nikola_Tesla http://en.wikipedia.org/wiki/Tesla_coil).

Unfortunately he couldn't avoid the leakage of energy which everyone mistook as something Tesla tried to achieve as wireless transmission of electricity. In fact, contrary to popular believe, Tesla never wanted to transmit wireless electricity as it is extremely (ENORMOUSLY) wasteful and inefficient, and by the way, the large solenoidal **generating coil** is actually both primary and secondary, where thick tubular "pancake" winding is known as "pick-up" coil, "transforming" extremely high voltage into high amps. And the story about not being able to put meter is also false because capitalist would always find a way to get his/her money (for example thru taxation) and there are ways to put meters even on wireless consumption. The concept of generating electricity without mechanical motion using only one coil is **deceptively** simple and uses well understood phenomenon known as Back EMF (electromotive force). Whenever we apply electricity to a wire it flows like "dominos" in chain reaction falling one by one (http://en.wikipedia.org/wiki/Serial_communication), but as soon as we disconnect it from source all "dominos" standing back up, all at once (http://en.wikipedia.org/wiki/Parallel_communication) and at much greater speed (pressure)! Thus, we have same amperage (as it was applied) flowing back but at much-much higher voltage. You can also compare it to a slow push forward and short (quick) powerful punch back. This technique actually being used in old CRT (cathode ray tube) monitors and the device is known as flyback transformer. (http://en.wikipedia.org/wiki/Flyback_transformer http://en.wikipedia.org/wiki/Cathode_ray_tube)

Obviously, all transformers currently in use are consuming more electricity than they generate. This is partly because they are being designed and used this way, whether it is unintentional or not. Just as with mechanical generators under load, transformers have to deal with tugging "war" of polarities and oppositely flowing currents, because generating coil under load (closed circuit) becomes electromagnet but with opposing magnetic polls, generating oppositely flowing current on the primary coil, thus creating friction and magnetic "brakes". As you know, friction (resistance) creates heat which is also wasteful leakage of energy. I personally (and by far not the first nor last) conducted experiments using "of the shelf" transformers where they would generate much more electricity than applied, by finding resonant frequency between primary and secondary coils, and those transformers never heated. As Tesla discovered, high (resonant) frequency and high voltage creates its own set of problems resulting in other losses of energy. Yes, it is possible to create small scale devices which would power itself and payload (a house or a car) using mechanically "motionless" transformer-generator, but for the industrial scales you'll need mass, and that means mechanical motion throughout massive magnetic fields. However, instead of using brute force to overcome "magnetic brakes" it is possible to use the Power-of-Stop also known as Zero Point Energy, where ambient pressure, known as Space-Time, would replenish spent energy in any amounts. (http://en.wikipedia.org/wiki/Zero-point_energy)

2. Single Wire Power Transmission: (http://en.wikipedia.org/wiki/Single-wire_transmission_line)

On the drawing below you can see diagram for the single wire electrical **power** transmission.

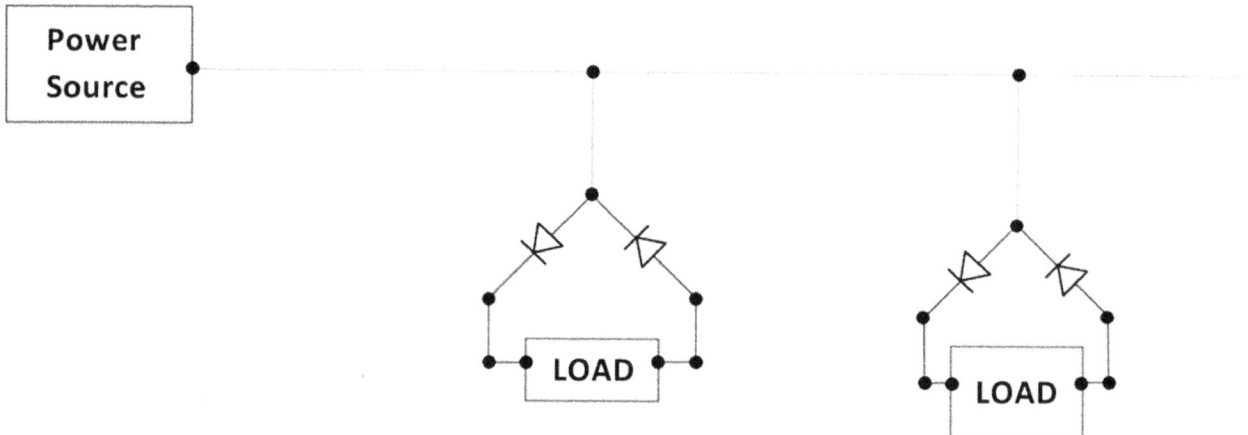

While this technique have been experimented by many people around the world (including Nicola Tesla), there are some confusions how and why it's working. The questions you should ask yourself are why it's only works at high frequencies and high voltages. Here we must debunk one of misleading perceptions about waves. If you actually read the theory and paid attention, you should know that waves are geometrically spherical and spiral in structure where depictions of waves as sine-wave or even square-wave are only an interpretation (an interface) as stated in chapter "Introduction". There is also confusion about supposedly "dividing" zero point (line). Actually, in waves there is no such thing as zero. That line is an indication of the equilibrium or half-point which equally divides wave on high (positively) saturated and low ("negatively") diffused regions. (Refer to chapters "Waves", "Motion-Information", "The Energy", "The Force", "Gravity", "Magnetism", "Electricity", "Light", "Space-Time" and "The Bridge")

The answer on above questions very simple and it has to do with full wave. As you should know, the frequency and wavelength are inversely related, thus high frequency at very short wavelength is creating overall highly saturated energy environment. (In your home, where AC power is delivered at very low frequency and extremely long wavelength, the phase line could be viewed as pressurized water pipe and neutral line as unpressurized sewer line.)

As far as high voltage; it needed because very thin wire cannot carry high current, plus, voltage and amperage are interchangeable and supplied load needs **POWER**. If your load is **100 watts**, you can achieve it by having 100 volts by 1 amp. or 100,000 volts by 1 milliamp (0.001 amps).

As with everything, there are some drawbacks since high frequency and voltage creates energy leakage because wire itself no longer acts as carrier but more like guide where entire current flows on the surface along the conducting medium, and no amount of insulation would stop it. In my experiments all insulated wires would produce around them glowing bluish hue. By the way, long stretched wire would also work as generator of electricity, and work even better than coiled, because invisible magnetic flux (produced whenever electricity flows) does not interferes with each other, therefore energy is not delayed (stored like capacitor) as with tightly wound coils. In fact, both the inductor and capacitor (famous LC or tank circuit http://en.wikipedia.org/wiki/LC_circuit) work pretty much the same, as caps are made either by coiling "flat" strips of wire or like a layered "cakes". Yes, capacitors holding (storing) "charges" longer, but the underline principles are the same.

3. True Antigravity Device:

The reason I call it "True" Antigravity is because this theoretical system is working on restructuring surrounding Space-Time substance to provide (cancel out) oppositely (to the Earth gravity) flow of acceleration, thus first negating, and then, providing lift, where source of power and propellant would be the Space-Time itself. Just as chemically powered (rockets) or winged crafts achieving lift by creating pressure differences, the Space-Time could be similarly manipulated to create higher pressure under and lower (to overall) pressure above the flying apparatus. And if it sounds like warp propulsion and so called "free" energy device, that is because, just as with everything, the principles are the same, and only difference is quantity of power manipulated. By reducing Space-Time density (saturation) above the craft and increasing (squeezing) it under, we can achieve enough warping of Space-Time to render it weightless, and by applying more power (derived from surrounding Space-Time) same technology would also create propulsion. Basically, we are talking about a redirection of acceleration, where some of the "gravitational" acceleration "down", is redirected "up" to counteract itself, effectively neutralizing the force. As usual, there are some issues to work out, because, just as with electricity, gravity not only the acceleration, but also the mass, where two are interchangeable (please refer to Appendix "A.1"). We can convert mass into extremely high acceleration, but then, it would look and work like plasma EM Drive, producing exceptionally bright light and gamma radiation under the craft, and bright bluish glow above and around the vehicle, or build enormously large vessel (we are talking several miles in diameter), to redirect enough of "gravitational" mass where spacecraft would hover without any visible, and most importantly, radiant excesses. (http://en.wikipedia.org/wiki/EmDrive)

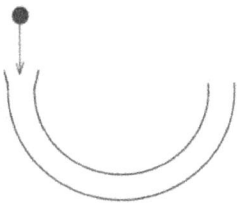

4. The Warp Propulsion:

In previous subsection it was mentioned, that so called "free" energy device, antigravity and warp propulsion are basically the same technology, and the only differences how much power is being applied (manipulated). However, due to misrepresentation by science fiction books, movies and cartoons; I have to point out that the warp drive is not about faster than speed of light acceleration, but actually about changing (warping) Space-Time itself, creating propulsion where Space-Time is both, source of energy and propellant. Theoretically, it would be possible to lower saturation of Space-Time in front of the craft so much, where surrounding Space-Time, rushing to equalize, would transport the spacecraft faster than speed of light **in relation** to Earth and Solar system, however, just because something is moving away extremely fast doesn't means it is actually traveling faster than speed of light. As stated by Albert Einstein and his relativity theories, you can measure something **ONLY** in relation to something else.

5. Instantaneous Communications:

The following explanation would appear to come out directly of the "Holographic Universe" theory and will be using somewhat "flat" impressions.

Suppose we got flat sheet of paper (two-dimensional substance) with embossed geometrical shapes. On one side of the "paper" some shapes are pushed-out, which means on the other side they are recessed. Let take the embossing into extreme and picture those shapes as pushed-out far-far away from the main body of the "sheet", while continuing being connected to it. Because the connecting parts of the "sheet" had to stretch so much, it exists at such low density (saturation) that we can't even detect it. However, the pushed-out shapes themselves are very physical and evident (approachable) to us, especially if some of them are being "reshaped" (squeezed) into smaller denser packages. In all this very hypothetical discussion we must not forget about the other side of our imaginary expanse, where those same shapes are recessed, "replaced" by so called "empty" geometry, and therefore non-existing as physical objects, and yet, recognizable, but as only and "pure" information. The described scenario can NOT be taken literally and meant only to help visualize possibility of instantaneous travel to any part of the universe by simply "switching" from recessed to embossed (pushed-out) presence, also known as "stepping through..." That is how all "objects" in the universe are connected and present (in the form of absence) everywhere and nowhere-in-particular. http://en.wikipedia.org/wiki/Quantum_tunnelling
Einstein–Rosen bridge http://en.wikipedia.org/wiki/Wormhole

6. Power of Subconscious Mind:

We all heard about power of suggestion and hypnosis. If you bothered to actually read or, even better, study the section "Book 1 Prologue", it should be very apparent by now just how much our subconscious mind controlling not only our thoughts but also actual physical body, including all sensory perceptions. It is well known fact, that thru exercise, meditation and strong believes (not talking about religious) people can actually cure themselves of practically any illness, including cancer, bad vision, diabetes and many more... It is well documented medical fact that placebo (basically sugar pills) helped patients to overcome physical as well as mental adversities beating "impossible" odds and gruesome predictions. As mentioned in "Book 1 Prologue" I have two dogs, male shepherd and female lab and pit-bull mix. At some point, while writing this book, I decided to grow beard and mustache, and obviously they are full of gray spots. To my enormous surprise after several months both of my dogs developed gray areas on same places as me. Have you ever notice that yawning travels from person to person and even from people to animals and vise-versa.

Appendix B: Antimatter Galaxies.

What you'll read here under "Appendix B" could be considered as wild guess, as I have absolutely no proof of this hypothesis and no perceptible technique to even test it in order to confirm or at least theoretically calculate virtues of the approach.

Before we begin I hope you do realize that all the pictures and videos of "Black-Holes" and Galaxies you have ever seen are not actual photographs, but more or less educated artistic rendering partly based on the expectations and partly on how those are viewed or envisioned by physicists, astronomers and cosmologists. All those famous "Hubble Telescope" deep and ultra-deep images where taken in near infrared spectra, and for you to enjoy saturated by visible color "photo" someone had to spend a lot of hours assigning colors by the chemical elements atomic masses and their redshift values. It is very important to keep this in mind because just as with everything, our perception is deceiving us especially when we dealing with large sized curvatures of Space-Time, as we judge straightness of visible lines by

photons (waves of light) traveling to our eyes, where in actuality those photons will follow curvatures of Space-Time as they are propagating using structure of the Space-Time as chain links or "falling dominos".

(Please refer to chapters "Waves" & "Light".) On the image you can see artistic depiction of the Earth magnetic field protecting us from solar and cosmic radiations. It is very easy to calculate the size of that field and how far it extends. As you know from cosmology, our planet by far not the biggest out there and its magnetic field also is not the strongest. Just consider how much larger it is of the planet Jupiter (http://en.wikipedia.org/wiki/Magnetosphere_of_Jupiter) and move on stars and other super large and enormously powerful objects like super massive "Black-Holes".

Those objects could be several billion times larger than our Sun and their magnetic fields would be even vaster as its power cubically proportional to the spinning mass.

The point I'm trying to make is that enormously powerful "Black-Holes", which are found at the center of all galaxies, would have magnetic fields so large (and curved Space-Time so deceptive) where entire galaxy would actually "sit" on top of one of the magnetic polls extending seemingly spiral "arms" down, following magnetic lines. If this wildly unprovable conjecture is true, then there is a good possibility that

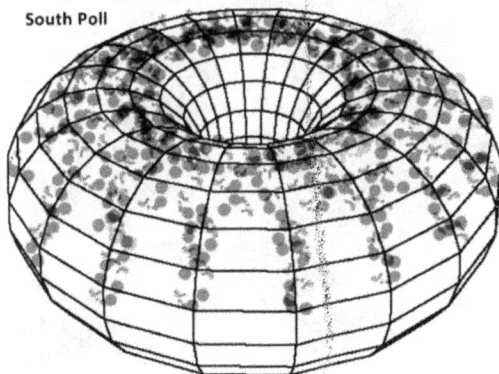

antimatter galaxies are "sitting" on the opposite magnetic poll extending its "arms" toward the mid-point where traveling light and other radiations are simply annihilating each other thus appearing to us as blobs of so called dark matter. I understand that this conclusion refutes my previous claims of dark matter being simply concentrated "clouds" of Space-Time, but if you take into consideration that all masses are collected and squeezed "lumps" of Space-Time at various phases, that assertion is accurate.

(Refer to chapters "Gravity", "Mass & Matter", "Mycelium Field Universe" and "Inside the Cocoon".) Whether this science-fictionally approach is worth to consider or not, it makes able scenario for a screenplay where evil antimatter aliens in magnetically or otherwise protective devices trying to take over the entire galaxy, and being stopped by humble earthlings, as usual against impossible odds, by huge matter-antimatter explosion. And yes, this is an attack on the recurring cliché where people of Earth are prevailing despite impossible odds against alien (or otherwise) enemies with vastly advanced technologies. Let us not forget that Spanish conquistadors of several hundred succeeded to decimate, occupy and forcibly convert population worth tens of millions in South America, possessing only slightly more advanced technologies in weapons and deception. I have to argue that any creatures being able to traverse such huge distances would have technologies so far beyond our capabilities where we not only be denied the very possibility to obtain targets to attack, but won't even realize that Earth is being conquered. That and other false perceptions are practically forced on peoples' minds so much that it is hard not to wander if that is intentional or not. In any case, since this books' entire discussion is about falsified perceptions and as result **misleading expectations**, I urge you to reevaluate many aspects in your quest to understand physical reality, as well as views on everyday seemingly trivial perceptions.

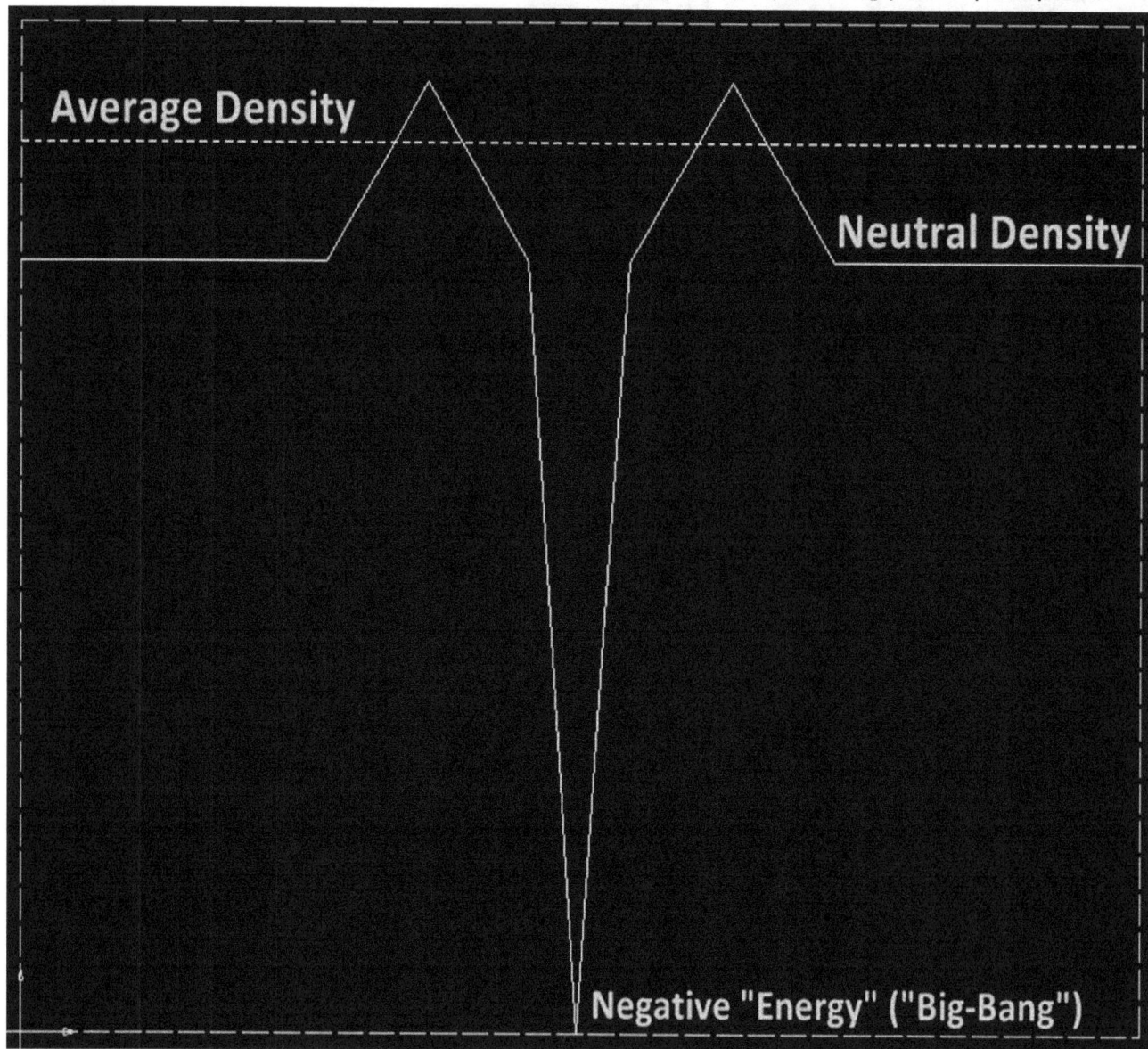

www.ingramcontent.com/pod-product-compliance
Lightning Source LLC
Chambersburg PA
CBHW081522040426
42447CB00013B/3311